IT'S A
GOD
THING

And Other Popular
Christian Misconceptions

IT'S A GOD THING

And Other Popular Christian Misconceptions

JIM DYET

Victor®

The Bible Teacher's Teacher

COOK COMMUNICATIONS MINISTRIES
Colorado Springs, Colorado • Paris, Ontario
KINGSWAY COMMUNICATIONS LTD
Eastbourne, England

Victor® is an imprint of
Cook Communications Ministries, Colorado Springs, CO 80918
Cook Communications, Paris, Ontario
Kingsway Communications, Eastbourne, England

IT'S A GOD THING AND OTHER POPULAR CHRISTIAN
MISCONCEPTIONS
© 2006 by Jim Dyet

The Web addresses (URLs) recommended throughout this book are
solely offered as a resource to the reader. The citation of these Web
sites does not in any way imply an endorsement on the part of the
author or the publisher, nor does the author or publisher vouch for
their content for the life of this book.

Cover Design: Marks & Whetstone
Cover Photo Credit: © iStockPhoto

First Printing, 2006
Printed in the United States of America

1 2 3 4 5 6 7 8 9 10 Printing/Year 11 10 09 08 07 06

Unless otherwise noted, Scripture quotations are taken from the *Holy
Bible, New International Version*®. *NIV*®. Copyright © 1973, 1978, 1984 by
International Bible Society. Used by permission of Zondervan. All
rights reserved. Scripture quotations marked KJV are taken from the
King James Version of the Bible. (Public Domain.) Italics in Scripture
have been added by the author for emphasis.

ISBN-13: 978-0-7814-4289-3
ISBN-10: 0-7814-4289-3

LCCN: 2006927276

To daughters Sherrie Escue and Heather Whiting and son Brian. They never wandered from their biblical beliefs and never lost their sense of humor.

CONTENTS

Appendixes are available online for free download and reproduction at
www.cookministries.com/misconceptions.
(Appendixes A and E are referenced in this book; appendixes B–D
engage misconceptions about the end-times.)

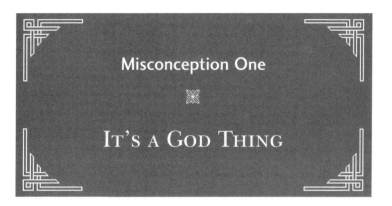

Misconception One

※

IT'S A GOD THING

I n spite of the popular belief that men are from Mars and women are from Venus, many couples get along quite well. Some even stay married for more than sixty years. But any couple can tell you some differences never change.

Take shopping, for example. A man shops only out of necessity. He may be down to his last dress shirt, and its collar is frayed. So he hops into his car, drives to a department store, walks briskly to the dress shirt display, finds his size, picks up a shirt, pays for it, hops back into his car, and returns home. It's a guy thing.

When a woman goes shopping, it isn't necessarily because she needs something. For her, shopping is a happening. It's like visiting a free museum. Upon entering the store, she looks for sales signs. If a sign at the Petites display announces "50% Off," she heads straight toward it. The "50% Off" draws her like a magnet. It doesn't matter that she is six feet tall. After shuffling pants and tops around in rack after rack, she moves on to another attraction, and another, and another.

Another difference: When have you seen two men shopping together? Women, on the other hand, often shop in twos or threes. And when one finds an item she likes, she shows it to her friend. Immediately, the two launch into a litany of girl talk. "So cute!" "Precious!" "How darling!" Can you imagine those words coming out of a guy's mouth?

And another difference: A husband and wife can eat lunch together at the same restaurant, but each one's focus is entirely different. His attention is riveted on the food. Hers is fixed on the couple at the next table. He is hardly aware there is a next table. After lunch, she tells him what each person at the next table was wearing, what they ordered, what they were talking about, and what their after-lunch plans were. She isn't nosy, just observant. It's a woman thing!

We have grown accustomed to hearing, "It's guy thing" or "It's a girl thing," and I suppose we can live with these remarks and the differences that prompt them. Recently, however, a spin-off comment has slipped into our Christian vocabulary, and I think we should bid it farewell. "It's a God thing" seems to explain every good turn of events that pops up in the Christian life.

Perhaps you have heard this expression in response to a situation like one of the following:

- ※ "There I was, driving 65 miles an hour down the freeway, when the front left tire blew out. I couldn't control the steering. Before I knew what was happening, I found myself skidding into the grassy median. I thought for sure I would crash into oncoming traffic, but my car stayed in the median and stopped just inches short of a culvert. A couple of motorists saw what happened and stopped to check on me. They said they were sure I was going to end up in a wreck and be killed. I told them I thought I would get killed too. Now, as I look back on what happened, I know my survival was a God thing!"

- ※ "Kim and I know every fertility specialist in the city, and every one of them said the possibility of our getting pregnant and having our own baby was about nil to zilch. But you know what? They were wrong. Four months from now we'll be singing 'Rock-a-Bye-Baby' to our own little guy. It's a God thing!"

- ※ "Greg and I had dreamed about owning a five-bedroom two-story house on a wooded lot backing onto a lake, but it was only a dream. We don't play the lottery, so there was no way we could come up with the money for our dream home. But the strangest thing happened. Last week the CEO called Greg into his office. It seems he had been getting good reports about Greg's ability to schedule products and ensure their quality. So he told Greg the company plans to build a second company in Oshkosh, Wisconsin, just a mile off Lake Winnebago. Here's where the story gets really good. The CEO wants Greg to be vice president of production and quality control at the new facility at a starting salary of $180,000. Dream house on the lake, here we come. It's a God thing. Oh, one more God thing—an exciting Bible-believing church is under construction right down the road from Greg's new workplace."

The health clinic called Maryann and asked her to return for another mammogram. The first had revealed a suspicious spot on her left breast. Maryann was worried. Did she have cancer? Surely God would not allow that to happen to a mother of one-year-old twin boys! She was too young and far too energetic to have cancer. She worked out every day, ate right, and pushed the boys in a twin stroller every day around a big neighborhood park.

The second mammogram followed by a biopsy confirmed the presence of an aggressive cancer. Both Maryann's physician and her surgeon explained her options. It seemed a radical mastectomy was the best option. A thorough pre-op examination would tell the full story.

Amazingly, the pre-op exam revealed no abnormality—no spot, no lump. Everything was suddenly normal. The medical staff could not offer an explanation. But Maryann could. "It's a God thing," she said with a bright smile.

Obviously, God cares for his children and causes good things to happen in our lives. But would the individuals mentioned in the preceding stories say, "It's a God thing" if the outcomes had been quite different? Let's revisit each story and turn the tables around.

- "There I was, driving 65 miles an hour down the freeway, when the front left tire blew out. I couldn't control the steering. Before I knew what was happening, I found myself skidding into the grassy median. I thought for sure I would crash into oncoming traffic, but my car stayed in the median and slammed into a culvert. I lost consciousness. When I came to, I was in Memorial Hospital. A neurologist told me I had been in a coma for three weeks. An orthopedic surgeon explained he had performed three surgeries to repair my shattered kneecaps, a broken right leg, and a broken pelvis. I might begin physical therapy soon, he said, but I might never walk again without assistance. Guess I'll have to get used to crutches and then graduate to a cane." *A God thing?*

※ "Kim and I know every fertility specialist in the city, and they all said the odds of our getting pregnant and having our own baby were nil to zilch. We hoped they were wrong, but after eight years of trying to get pregnant, it seems they were right. Looks like we'll never get to sing 'Rock-a-Bye-Baby' to our own little guy or girl. Friends say we should adopt a child, but we simply don't want to." *A God thing?*

※ "Greg and I had dreamed about owning a five-bedroom two-story house on a wooded lot backing onto a lake, but it was only a dream. Last Friday, Greg got called into his manager's office. It seems the company's profit line has dipped every year for the past five years, so the company decided to lay Greg and a bunch of other middle managers off. The boss told Greg to clean out his desk and go home. Now what are we going to do? Greg received only one month's severance pay, and jobs in his field are almost nonexistent. We can kiss our dream house good-bye. We may not even be able to pay the rent on our apartment much longer. Instead of living a dream, we're now living a night-mare!" *A God thing?*

※ The health clinic had called Maryann and asked her to return for another mammogram. The first had revealed a suspicious spot on her left breast.

Maryann was worried. Did she have cancer? Surely God would not allow that to happen to a mother of one-year-old twin boys! She was too young and far too energetic to have cancer. She worked out every day, ate right, and pushed the boys in a twin stroller every day around a big neighborhood park.

The second mammogram followed by a biopsy confirmed the presence of an aggressive cancer. Both Maryann's physician and her surgeon explained her options. It seemed a radical mastectomy was the best option.

That was ten months ago. Maryann had the surgery and hoped to resume normal, energetic life. Her husband has been supportive, and the twins are now walking and acting like most two-year-old boys. But Maryann is troubled. Cancer has returned and is attacking both her liver and her brain. In all likelihood, she has only three or four months to live. When she dies, she will leave behind a grieving husband and two lonely, confused little boys. *A God thing?*

When my two brothers and I were wee laddies, our Scottish mither (mother) gave us cod-liver oil regularly. We screwed up our noses and turned our heads every time she put a spoonful of the stuff near our mouths, but our faither (father) would order: "You get that knocked into ye, or I'll break baith [both] your legs." Strict child protection laws didn't exist back then, and a swig of cod-liver oil seemed more desirable than two broken legs, so my brothers and I downed what was supposed to be good for us.

Sometimes we Christians screw up our noses and try to turn away from distasteful circumstances. We can't possibly imagine that our loving heavenly Father wants us to experience such distasteful things as pain and suffering, financial hardship, or loneliness. Such "bad" things certainly aren't his things, are they? In other words, when good fortune enters our lives, we say it's a God thing, but when ill fortune invades our lives, we say the Devil is out to get us.

Perhaps we need an attitude adjustment.

The apostle Paul didn't get wealthy; he got welts. In 2 Corinthians 11 he reported, "I have … been flogged … severely…. Five times I received from the Jews the forty lashes minus one. Three times I was beaten with rods, once I was stoned" (vv. 23–25). His life was never smooth sailing; he experienced rough seas and shipwreck (see Acts 27). He never spent a day in a penthouse; however, he spent many nights in prison. No one ever threw him a party; most of his friends deserted him (2 Tim. 4:16). Instead of everything coming up roses for Paul, he received a "thorn in [the] flesh" (2 Cor. 12:7). His only stocks were iron stocks that secured him in prison (Acts 16:24). When his life ended, he wasn't rolling in money; his head was rolling across an executioner's floor. Yet this same man, Paul, trumpeted the truth that "we know that in all things God works for the good of those who love him, who have been called according to his purpose" (Rom. 8:28).

This amazing truth comes alive when we understand God's purpose for us is to conform us "to the likeness of his Son" (Rom. 8:29). If we truly want to be like Jesus, we must experience friction and buffeting. Tough times can help make our hearts tender, our lives pure, and our faith strong. The apostle Peter taught us to see trials as having greater value than gold. They refine our faith and prove its genuineness (1 Peter 1:6–7). James even advised us to "consider it pure joy" when we "face trials of many kinds" (James 1:2). He urged us to anticipate the results of such testing—spiritual maturity (vv. 3–4).

Long before Romans, 1 Peter, and James were written, men like Job, Joseph, and David learned to view "all things" as fulfilling God's plan for their lives.

If the expression "It's a God thing" had been circulating in Job's day, some of Job's friends might have used it to explain his enormous success. His ranch spread far enough to make Texas cattlemen envious. His flocks and herds dotted the landscape like ants on a discarded slice of watermelon. He and his wife owned a number of homes and enjoyed the good life. Their seven sons and three daughters thrived on the rich land. So did his many ranch hands. Everything was as close to perfect as it could be, including Job's spiritual life.

But suddenly that good life turned ugly. Lightning strikes, a tornado-force wind, and marauders reduced Job's livestock to nothing and killed most of his ranch hands and all of his sons and daughters. Then Job's health went south. He experienced excruciating pain and crushing emotional distress. His so-called friends credited all the bad events to sin in Job's life, and his wife rubbed salt on his wounds by telling him to curse God and die. No one said, "It's a God thing!"

The rest of the story vindicates Job. He maintained his faith. He testified he would still hope in God even if God were to slay him (Job 13:15). He looked beyond life on earth to life in the glory of the resurrection, believing he would behold his Redeemer with his own eyes (19:25–27). When all the trials finally lifted, Job's view of God's character and ways was richer and fuller than before the trials rained down on him. Troubles had not made Job bitter; they had made him better. They had given him a better understanding of his mortality and humanness and a greater appreciation of God's majesty and wisdom.

The whole story of Job's suffering includes a behind-the-scenes look at spiritual forces. We learn that Satan, the Devil, whined to God that Job worshipped and obeyed God only because God had blessed Job so abundantly. He claimed Job would curse God if God swept away everything from Job (1:11). God knew Job better than Satan knew Job. God knew trials would only validate Job's faith and draw Job closer to him, so he allowed Satan to assault Job. However, he restrained Satan from taking Job's life. The drama ended with a defeated Satan, a vindicated Job, and a victorious God!

We may not like trials, but they serve us well. When we are flat on our backs, we are looking up! We pray with a sense of urgency, and we search the Bible diligently for reasons and promises. Patience builds stronger roots of faith, and the fruit of the Spirit flourishes in our attitudes and actions.

Nearly a third of the book of Genesis is devoted to the story of Joseph. When he was a youngster, he received a multicolored coat from his father. It distinguished him as Dad's favorite of the twelve sons. He also received a couple of dreams from God that predicted he would be prominent. According to the dreams, Joseph's parents and brothers would pay him homage. So Joseph could have summed it all up as "It's a God thing." But he didn't!

As he grew older, Joseph encountered trouble on top of trouble. From a purely human perspective it seemed like his life was caving in like a poorly constructed building struck by a 6.5 earthquake. His brothers nearly killed him but sold him into slavery instead. He was taken far from home by traders to Egypt and sold to a high-ranking military officer. The officer's wife tried desperately and repeatedly to seduce Joseph; when her efforts failed, she framed him, charging him with attempted rape. Joseph received a prison sentence, and Egyptian prison life was extremely tough.

Who would call any of Joseph's "tragedies" a God thing? But years later, when all his "tragedies" were only memories and Joseph was the Pharaoh's right-hand man, Joseph reconciled with his brothers and declared: "You intended to harm me, but God intended it for good" (Gen. 50:20).

Get the picture? It's better than the best Kodak moment. God designs everything in our lives for our good and his glory.

If you have spent much time reading King David's psalms, you will get an enlarged copy of this grand picture. He wrote most of his psalms after experiencing persecution and deprivation. They originated from desert caves and other hiding places, not from the comfort of a royal palace. They rendered praise to God during hard times, as they acknowledged his presence and provision.

Even Psalm 23, which begins on a tranquil note, reflects on God's presence and provision in hard times. Have you noticed the use of the third-person pronoun in verses 2 and 3? David wrote: "*He* makes me lie down in green pastures, *he* leads me beside quiet waters, *he* restores my soul. *He* guides me in paths of righteousness for *his* name's sake." Suddenly, David reflected on trouble and trials and switched to the second-person pronoun. "Even though I walk through the valley of the shadow of death, I will fear no evil, for *you* are with me; *your* rod and *your* staff, they comfort me. *You* prepare a table before me in the presence of my enemies. *You* anoint my head with oil; my cup overflows" (vv. 4–5).

There's no doubt about it, we can look upon tough circumstances as launching pads to a closer relationship with the Lord. So why should we single out only what we see as a fortuitous turn of events as "a God thing"?

Something else to consider: The construction "It's a God thing" employs "God" as an adjective, and an adjective is less important than the noun it modifies.

How would you like to be referred to as an adjective modifying a thing? It would certainly depersonalize you. Saying, "It's a Mary or a Craig or a Dan thing," makes Mary, Craig, or Dan less important than the "thing" referred to. Therefore, it seems to me the adjectival use of God's name diminishes respect and reverence for him.

By contrast, God's name deserves our highest esteem. We should not mention it lightly or thoughtlessly. Exodus 20:7 commands, "You shall not misuse the name of the Lord your God," and Jesus taught us to hallow God's name (Matt. 6:9). We may not intend any disrespect for

God's name when we say, "It's a God thing," but unintentional error is error nonetheless.

Here's a sure way to gather a crowd. Stand on a busy sidewalk and stare into the sky. Before long a crowd of pedestrians will join you. Everyone in the crowd will peer into the empty sky to find what you are looking at. Because many Christians are followers—groupies—they quickly pick up on popular expressions, even empty ones like "It's a God thing." Soon a big crowd is exclaiming, "It's a God thing."

Isn't it time to drop this unscriptural expression and leave mob mentality behind?

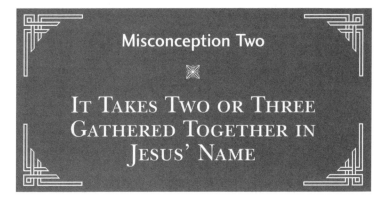

IT TAKES TWO OR THREE GATHERED TOGETHER IN JESUS' NAME

I t was the same old same old. Like every Wednesday evening at seven, Jack and Carol Woolford, Debbie Morgan, Molly Jefferson, and Pastor Bill and his wife, Sue, had arranged several chairs in a circle in the church's basement and were quietly awaiting the start of the weekly prayer service. The downcast expression on Pastor Bill's face spoke volumes. Clearly, he was discouraged by the congregation's lack of interest in the midweek prayer service. Jack peered around the room, wondering once again why so many members chose to stay home. *They must be addicted to TV,* he thought. Then he glanced at Pastor Bill. Sensing the pastor's discouragement, he intoned, "I don't know why our group is so small, but the Lord promised that where two or three are gathered together in his name, there he would be in the midst of them."

~ 23 ~

Jack was probably more aware of the absence of the many than he was of the presence of the Lord in the midst of the few, but was his observation valid? Did he correctly apply the promise of Matthew 18:20 to the situation at hand, or was he off the mark? And just what does it take to acquire the Lord's presence?

Did Jack correctly apply the promise of Matthew 18:20? The context surrounding this verse holds the answer.

If you read Matthew 18:15–20, you will discover at a glance that this context doesn't relate to a midweek prayer service. The situation it describes isn't nearly as chummy as a prayer service. Quite the opposite! The situation bristles with tension and crackles with conflict. It involves sin, an offended believer, one or two witnesses, and a congregation's decision to excommunicate the guilty party. Jesus was preparing his disciples for leadership in the first-century church. Knowing that personal conflicts would arise in local assemblies of believers, he counseled, "If your brother sins against you, go and show him his fault, just between the two of you. If he listens to you, you have won your brother over" (v. 15).

Generally, believers ought to be able to settle their differences quietly, peaceably, and agreeably. After all, they belong to the same spiritual family, share common beliefs and values, want to please their heavenly Father, and understand that love covers a multitude of sins. So the counsel Jesus gave in verse 15 ought to mend a broken fence, shouldn't it?

Of course! But sometimes only the offended person wants to repair the fence. While he works to put the boards back into place, the person who caused the damage keeps kicking them out.

For example, Kip had an affair with Hank's wife, Caitlin. It all started as a flirting session between the two in the choir room. Then, after a choir practice, Kip and Caitlin went out for coffee. Soon, they were meeting for more than coffee—at a motel. When Caitlin could no longer live with her stabbing conscience, she confessed her sin to Hank and asked for his forgiveness. She said she had called off the affair with Kip, but he would not give up. Instead, he was pleading with her to stay in the illicit relationship. She also expressed a willingness to confess her transgression before the whole church and ask for forgiveness.

Caitlin's shocking news stunned and angered Hank, but he found the grace to forgive her. Then he decided to confront Kip. At first, Hank railed against Kip, but then he calmed down and urged Kip to confess his wrongdoing and break off all communication with Caitlin. He even offered to forgive Kip if he would admit his sin and agree to leave Caitlin alone. However, Kip showed no remorse. Instead, he cursed Hank and threatened to punch out his lights if he raised the subject again.

~ 25 ~

Now, what was Hank to do? Jesus' further instruction dictates: "But if he will not listen, take one or two others along, so that every matter may be established by the testimony of two or three witnesses" (v. 16). Obviously, Jesus valued the Old Testament principle of establishing truth at the mouth of two or three witnesses. He honored Deuteronomy 19:15: "One witness is not enough to convict a man accused of any crime or offense he may have committed. A matter must be established by the testimony of two or three witnesses."

Hank took the next step. Accompanied by three members of the church board, he confronted Kip about the affair and begged him to leave Caitlin alone. At first, Kip denied the accusation, but denial turned to rage. He admitted the affair but once again threatened to rough Hank up if he didn't stop hounding him.

Hank and the others could only regret Kip's adamant spirit. Shaking their heads almost in disbelief, they walked away.

But the story doesn't end there. Jesus counseled that if a sinning brother refuses to listen to witnesses, they should "tell it to the church" (v. 17). Although no local churches existed when Jesus spoke these words, the word translated "church" can be applied to a church. The word means "assembly" and usually referred to an assembly of Jews, but it can also refer to a future assembly or congregation of church members. So in a church business meeting Hank and the three witnesses reported Kip's sin and the steps they had taken to restore him. They also reported that Kip had resisted every effort on their part. Prayerfully, the church determined its course of action. It officially contacted Kip, urged him to repent, and explained that he would be dropped from membership if he refused to comply.

Kip remained obstinate and unrepentant.

Having followed every step to restore Kip without resolving the conflict, the church dropped him from its membership. It had done what Jesus instructed: "If he refuses to listen even to the church, treat him as you would a pagan or a tax collector" (v. 17). Jesus would affirm the church's action, whether it resulted in forgiving and restoring a repentant member or excommunicating an unrepentant member (v. 18). He guaranteed, "If two of you on earth agree about anything you ask for, it will be done for you by my Father in heaven. For where two or three come together in my name [under my authority and meeting to protect my reputation], there am I with them" (vv. 19–20).

Church discipline is almost as extinct as dinosaurs. Why? Perhaps, we just don't have the stomach for it. It is unpleasant business. If we discipline an unrepentant, sinning church member, he will simply join a church across town, we reason. So what have we accomplished? Worse still, he may have relatives and friends in the church. If we take disciplinary action, they may get upset and leave the church. Perhaps, we fail to exercise church discipline because we misapply Jesus' promise to be with us when two or three have come together in his name. If we properly applied his promise, we might be confident that he is in charge of the disciplinary process instead of fearing a negative backlash.

Is Jesus with us only when we gather to exercise church discipline? No! He is with us all the time and everywhere we go, but we should not use Matthew 18:20 to prove the point. We can appeal to many other Scripture verses to attest to his abiding presence.

Jesus taught his disciples that he and the Father make their home with whoever loves and obeys him (John 14:23). When asked about our permanent residence, we give the address of our home. "Home" indicates permanence and comfort. Unlike a guesthouse or a hotel room, our home belongs to us and in turns gives us a sense of belonging. We furnish it for our personal enjoyment. It is a place where we can settle down and feel comfortable. So our hearts are Christ's home. He dwells there permanently. We may not always furnish our hearts to his liking, but he doesn't leave. However, we would do well to turn the designing and decorating over to him.

When Jesus commissioned his disciples to proclaim the good news throughout the world, he promised, "And surely I am with you always, to the very end of the age" (Matt. 28:20). How, then, can we doubt that he is with us?

Seated next to a guest speaker, the pastor of a rather emotional congregation whispered, "Surely, the Lord is with us this morning. I can feel his presence."

Recalling Jesus' promise to his disciples when he commissioned them to proclaim the good news worldwide, the guest speaker assured the pastor, "The Lord is with us, whether we feel his presence or not."

Indeed, he is with us—and not just when we meet as a church to exercise discipline.

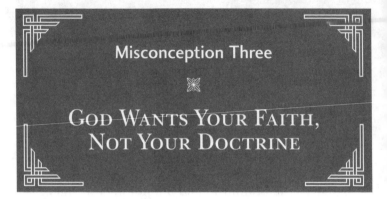

God Wants Your Faith, Not Your Doctrine

At the age of twenty-two I was eager to enter my first full-time pastorate. Pastoral training at Moody Bible Institute was under my belt and so was a major in religion at Houghton College in New York State. My pastoral experience was limited but varied. I had preached at Pacific Garden Mission in Chicago every Sunday morning during my last two and a half years at Moody. Also, I had opened a closed country church near Houghton College and had served as its pastor until I graduated. Because I held Canadian citizenship and was in the United States on a student visa, I had to return to Canada when Houghton College handed me a diploma. Five days later I entered another institution—marriage—and moved back to St. Catharines, Ontario, with Gloria, my bride from Virginia, at my side. I could hardly wait to become a full-time pastor, and I was sure my congregation would welcome strong doctrinal sermons.

Within a couple of months I received an invitation to

preach at a small town about twenty miles north of Toronto. The church needed a pastor and had learned of my availability from the interim pastor of my home church. It would be an understatement to say I poured prayer, zeal, and Theology 404 knowledge into a trial sermon. I planned to deliver a never-to-be-forgotten message on pneumatology, the doctrine of the Holy Spirit.

The special Sunday arrived. The sun was shining and birds were chirping. Crimson and yellow roses flanked the sidewalk entrance to the old church building. Its freshly coated white frame reflected the sun's rays. Everything was picture perfect. But once inside, I saw the positive picture turn negative. All it took was a sign in the foyer.

We have no creed but Christ. No law but love.

Hoping against hope that the sign was simply a warm, fuzzy alert to visitors that the church was nonthreatening, I asked the first person to greet Gloria and me, "Does your church have a printed doctrinal statement?"

Attempting a smile, he replied, "No, we don't. We don't think doctrine is important."

As I think back to that experience, almost everything after the conversation in the foyer left a blip in my mind's memory. I can recall two things, though: (1) When Gloria and I walked to our car after the service, the sun had slipped behind a dark cloud, the birds were chirping off-key, the roses were drooping, and (2) I did not receive a call to be the church's pastor.

A decade later I received a church profile and a pastoral candidate form from a suburban Chicago church. The congregation had built a reputation on strong interpersonal relationships, and its profile announced that it was "seeking a pastor who knew what he believed."

Aha! I'm the man, I thought. *I may not know everything, but I do know what I believe.*

I read on. "We want a pastor with settled theological beliefs, but we would strongly object to any attempt to persuade the congregation to his point of view. He will serve primarily as a resource person."

They don't want a pastor; they want a librarian, I mused as I filed the mailing under "Churches out of the Question."

The 1960s and 1970s witnessed popular gimmicks and giveaway contests in a segment of evangelical churches. Hoping to attract crowds and boost Sunday school attendance, those growth-minded churches gave away everything from trinkets to travel vouchers to students who brought the most visitors to Sunday school in a specified period of time. In their zeal for numbers, some pastors promised to swallow goldfish or preach on their church's rooftop or skydive into the church's parking lot or let students smash their faces with cream pies if Sunday school attendance reached a high goal. Although the dog and pony shows piled up new names on the Sunday school rolls, the additions soon rolled away to other churches in search of something that would help them grow spiritually. Many who promoted "the circus and carnival" growth methods eventually saw the methods' weakness, and in time the circuses and carnivals closed.

During the gimmicky era, a Christian education director in Louisiana was concerned that his congregation lacked Bible knowledge. Somehow, he succeeded in persuading the church's board to bring a few curriculum educators, including me, to his church. The senior pastor balked at the series of training workshops my colleagues and I had arranged for the Sunday school workers. He told those attending the Sunday morning service that Bible teaching wasn't for every church. His church, he said, was a soul-winning church, not a Bible-teaching church, so he wanted his Sunday school teachers to avoid implementing what they would hear from us about how to teach the Bible. After the admonition, he presented two live chickens to the person who had brought the most visitors to Sunday school the previous week. Obviously, his pluck outstripped his politeness.

Is our postmodern era better informed about Bible doctrine? Is there a strong desire today to know and apply Bible doctrine? I don't think so. It seems to me that many churches are being swept along in a landslide of emotionalism and care little about doctrine. Exceptions exist, of course, but often what matters is how people feel about themselves, their worship experience, and the church's programs. The popular buzz is, "Where is the best worship in town?" Long gone is the question, "Where is the best Bible teaching?" Is it any wonder Bible colleges and seminaries express their disappointment with incoming students' Bible knowledge test scores? Are we surprised that a paltry number of Christians carry a Bible to church? Why carry a Bible if there is no reason to open it?

Worship is truly important. The Bible instructs us to "worship the LORD in the splendor of his holiness" (Ps. 29:2), and Jesus assured us that God's "worshipers must worship in spirit and in truth" (John 4:24). Our worship, therefore, involves the prompting of the Holy Spirit in accordance with truth.

But what is truth?

A relativist would answer, "There is no absolute truth."

A postmodernist would say, "Truth is whatever you believe it is."

Jesus referred to God's Word as truth and asked his heavenly Father to sanctify us (make us holy) by the truth (John 17:17). And that's why Bible doctrine is so important. Doctrine is simply the teaching of God's Word, which, when properly understood and applied, makes us the kind of people God wants us to be.

What would we know about God and his purposes for our lives if it were not for what we have learned from the

Bible? The Bible's teaching—doctrine—communicates everything we need to know about him and his will that we cannot gain from natural revelation. Nature shows that God is highly intelligent, mighty, orderly, purposeful, and benevolent, but only the doctrine of God given in the Bible reveals his love, grace, mercy, faithfulness, transcendence, triune being, eternality, omnipresence, righteousness, forgiveness, holiness, justice, immutability (unchanging character), and truthfulness.

How would we know to respond to God in faith by trusting in Jesus as our Savior if it were not for the Bible doctrine of salvation? How would we know we could trust him to guide our lives if it were not for the Bible's teaching about his wisdom, care, and abiding presence? How would we know what a righteous God requires of us if it were not for the instruction the Bible imparts? How would we know what a wise and loving heavenly Father has planned for us if it were not for the Bible's teaching about the future?

The Greek word *didache*, translated "doctrine" in the New Testament, derives from the word *didasko*, meaning "I teach." *Didache* in the New Testament refers to the body of teaching—the truth—that Jesus and his apostles communicated to believers. Understandably, the believers who witnessed the formation of the church on the day of Pentecost "devoted themselves to the apostles' teaching [*didache*]" (Acts 2:42). Who can question the reality of the early believers' faith? Based on the apostles' doctrine, the early believers' faith was strong enough to attract thousands to Christ, forge a bond of close fellowship, endure severe persecution, and launch a vigorous relief program. Their doctrinal learning produced dynamic living.

The ancient Greeks associated *didache* (teaching) with on-the-job training or the teaching of skills. The word also meant to demonstrate a theory. Geometry students, for example, had to prove each theorem they had studied. Similarly, a working faith demonstrates that we have learned Bible doctrine.

Before becoming an apostle, Paul was Saul of Tarsus, a young firebrand persecutor of the church. He despised Jesus of Nazareth and all his followers. Acts 9:1 depicts him as "breathing out murderous threats against the Lord's disciples." He lived to eradicate the name and message of Jesus from the earth. Like so many religious zealots, he had funneled his devotion to religious tradition into hatred. His theological wires were crossed, and red-hot sparks were flying wildly as he journeyed from Jerusalem to Damascus in search of followers of Jesus. With arrest warrants in hand, Saul salivated for the taste of martyrs' blood, and he didn't care whether it flowed from the veins of men or women.

Nice man? Of course not! But he was sincere about what he believed. Unfortunately he was sincerely wrong.

His skewed doctrine (teaching) produced rabid conduct. Looking back on that period of life, Paul wrote in Galatians 1:13–14: "For you have heard of my previous way of life in Judaism, how intensely I persecuted the church of God and tried to destroy it. I was advancing in Judaism beyond many Jews of my own age and was extremely zealous for the traditions of my fathers."

Did you catch the word "traditions"? If Saul of Tarsus had heeded the Old Testament Scriptures, he would have learned the doctrine of Christ and the need to love God supremely and others as oneself. Faith in the Old Testament prophecies about Jesus Christ would have prepared Saul to believe in him, just as a number of devout Jews waiting for the consolation of Israel believed in Jesus (see Luke 1 and 2). But Saul allowed traditions to block truth.

Everything changed dramatically, though, when the risen Christ stopped Saul in his tracks on the road to Damascus. His glory blinded Saul, but Christ's grace flooded his heart with light. Saul believed in Christ and submitted his life to him. Soon after his conversion experience, he was alone in the Arabian Desert, learning the doctrines of grace from the Holy Spirit. He had entered the desert with a load of traditions on his back; he left with the gospel of grace in his heart. Emerging from the desert, he was ready to teach doctrine and lead a godly life.

Paul knew by firsthand experience that faith and doctrine are inseparable. Before his conversion, he had placed his faith in traditions and operated his life like a steaming locomotive running downhill off the rails. After his conversion, his faith, joined to correct doctrine, kept his life on the track God had set for him. He testified in 2 Corinthians 4:2 that he and his fellow workers set forth "the truth plainly" and commended themselves "to every man's conscience in the sight of God."

The Lord used the apostle Paul to write thirteen New Testament letters. Most of those letters were addressed to churches, while a few were addressed to individuals; but all are rich in doctrine and strong on application. A quick survey of Paul's letters clearly reveals that they summon us to show our faith by implementing doctrinal instruction.[1]

The link between doctrine and the implementation of real faith in Paul's letters is unmistakable, but it leaps at us from 2 Timothy 3:15–17. Paul credits the holy, God-breathed Scriptures as able to make us "wise for salvation through faith in Christ Jesus," to smooth the rough edges of our lives, to educate us "in righteousness," and to equip us "for every good work."

Where would we be without God's truth? How useless our "faith" would be if it did not spring from the soil of Scripture?

Paul wasn't the only apostle to link doctrine and real faith. The apostles Peter and John did the same thing in their letters. In his first letter, the apostle Peter instructed his persecuted readers about how suffering fulfills God's purpose—to approve and strengthen personal faith (1:3–9). Building on this theme, Peter identified Christ's sufferings as the perfect example of accepting God's will (2:21–24; 4:12–19). He also wrote about the glory Christ entered into after suffering and encouraged his readers to anticipate the glory that awaits all believers in heaven (5:10).

Writing 2 Peter, the apostle Peter taught that God has given believers everything they need to lead a godly life (1:3) and urged his readers to add noble virtues to their faith (vv. 5–7). He also instructed his readers about the end-times and exhorted: "What kind of people ought you to be? You ought to live holy and godly lives as you look forward to the day of God and speed its coming" (3:11–12). Having focused their sight on eternity, he reasoned, "So then, dear friends, since you are looking forward to this, make every effort to be found spotless, blameless and at peace with him" (v. 14).

All who argue that prophecy is unimportant place themselves at odds with Peter's inspired comments. An awareness of what lies ahead prods our faith to implement God's provisions for the present and to anticipate the fulfillment of God's plans for the future: "In keeping with his promise we are looking forward to a new heaven and a new earth, the home of the righteous" (2 Peter 3:13). In the meantime, we ought to "grow in the grace and knowledge of our Lord and Savior Jesus Christ" (v. 18).

The apostle John linked truth (doctrine) and practical Christian living. Throughout his first letter he identified the evidences of real faith as a righteous lifestyle and love for God and others. In 1 John 3:1–2 he focused his readers' attention on the amazing love God had lavished on his children and promised that we shall see Christ and be like him when he appears. Tying together the truth of the Lord's coming and the importance of becoming Christlike, John wrote, "Everyone who has this hope in him purifies himself, just as he is pure" (v. 3).

Who hasn't known someone who professed to be a believer and later succumbed to false teaching and joined a cult? Who hasn't witnessed someone's profession of faith and subsequent slide back into his or her former sinful lifestyle. Faith that is not anchored in doctrine leaves a person as vulnerable to the winds of false teaching and the currents of immoral conduct as a ship adrift on the high seas is vulnerable to destructive winds and swirling ocean currents. But the person who anchors his or her faith in sound doctrine stands firm in the face of every onslaught of error and temptation.

Is it any wonder the apostle Jude urged his readers to "contend for the faith [Bible doctrine] that was once for all entrusted to the saints" (Jude v. 3) and concluded his letter by challenging them to "build yourselves up in your most holy faith" (v. 20)?

I am sure no one has ever seen a boxcar pulling a train. Engines pull trains. Like a boxcar, faith is incapable of taking life in the direction God has mapped for it unless it is connected to the engine of biblical truth. Truth empowers our faith and takes it where God wants it to go. Believers and congregations cannot go wrong by linking doctrine (biblical truth) and faith.

Misconception Four

Beware the Unpardonable Sin!

Every Thanksgiving Eve the president of the United States pardons his main course—a turkey—usually assigning it to a petting farm, where children lavish plenty of TLC on it. The tradition started with Harry S. Truman and has become popular. More serious, of course, are presidential pardons or the granting of amnesty to such notorious figures as the Whiskey Rebellion rebels in 1795, Confederate rebels in 1868, Richard Nixon in 1974, Tokyo Rose in 1977, Vietnam draft resisters in 1977, Caspar Weinberger in 1992, Edwin L. Cox Jr. in 1993, and Marc Rich in 2001.

We may wonder why a president would grant a pardon in a given situation, but we cannot question his authority to do so. Our main concern focuses on pardon for our own offenses, the vast majority of which seem trivial but are troubling nonetheless. Will my wife forgive me for coming home late from bowling or for playing golf on my day off instead of doing yard work? Will my husband forgive me for refusing to attend his company's Christmas party? Will my mother-in-law forgive me for the mean thing I said against her in a moment of anger? Will the boss forgive me for calling in sick, only to run into me at the ball game? Will the pastor forgive me for falling asleep during last Sunday's sermon?

Finding forgiveness for such offenses brings genuine relief, doesn't it? Forgiveness works like a soothing salve for the soul. But, even if a spouse or mother-in-law or boss refuses to forgive, our guilt may diminish with the passing of time. But some offenses are so heinous that those who commit them believe they can never be forgiven or relieved of heavy guilt. They believe they have committed the unpardonable sin. Do they have legitimate reason to worry?

Jesus referred to a sin that cannot be forgiven in Matthew 12, Mark 3, and Luke 12. He said:

> I tell you, every sin and blasphemy will be forgiven men, but the blasphemy against the Spirit will not be forgiven. Anyone who speaks a word against the Son of Man will be forgiven, but anyone who speaks against the Holy Spirit will not be forgiven, either in this age or in the age to come. (Matt. 12:31–32)
>
> I tell you the truth, all the sins and blasphemies of men will be forgiven them. But whoever blasphemes against the Holy Spirit will never be forgiven; he is guilty of an eternal sin. (Mark 3:28–29)

> I tell you, whoever acknowledges me before men, the Son
> of Man will also acknowledge him before the angels of
> God. But he who disowns me before men will be dis-
> owned before the angels of God. And everyone who
> speaks a word against the Son of Man will be forgiven, but
> anyone who blasphemes against the Holy Spirit will not
> be forgiven. (Luke 12:8–10)

These words carry a heavy message that resonates with authority and involves the eternal destiny of the soul. If we examine the context in which Jesus spoke about the unpardonable sin, we will understand what he meant. Hopefully, this understanding will clear up some common misconceptions and allow those who hold them to escape an unbearable sense of guilt.

I asked members of a biblically literate congregation to write what they believed to be the unpardonable sin. Their answers varied. Here are the most frequent responses:

- rejecting Jesus as Savior;
- saying Jesus is not the Son of God and dying with that belief;
- suicide;
- cursing the Lord;
- mistreating your spouse;
- denying Christ and his finished work;
- attributing the work of the Holy Spirit to Satan;
- lying about your faith to others;

- ✱ continually rejecting Jesus until your heart becomes too hard to respond to him;
- ✱ lying about what you believe so others will accept you;
- ✱ taking the Lord's Supper unworthily.

As you can see, these interpretations cover a broad spectrum, but they can't all be right. Before we examine the biblical context in which Jesus spoke of a sin that will never be forgiven, we can dispense with several interpretations listed above as viable interpretations.

The Bible says very little about suicide, and it never indicates that suicide bars a person from heaven. Samson committed suicide by collapsing a pagan temple onto the heads of his enemies, the Philistines. He even prayed that the Lord would let him die with the Philistines (Judg. 16:30). The Bible doesn't indicate that the Lord barred Samson from heaven because he took his own life.

King Saul committed suicide by falling on his own sword after Philistine archers had wounded him critically. He chose suicide because he wanted to escape death by torture at the hands of the Philistines (1 Sam. 31:1–4). Again, the Bible does not say that suicide disqualified him from life in heaven. After Saul committed suicide, his armor bearer also committed suicide by falling on his own sword (v. 5), but no comment follows that suggests suicide doomed him eternally.

The Bible records three other suicides, two without any comment about the suicide victims' eternal fate, and the third with an earlier reference indicating he was not a believer. The two are Ahithophel (2 Sam. 17:23) and Zimri (1 Kings 16:18). The third is Judas (Matt. 27:5; Acts 1:18), identified as "the one doomed to destruction" (John 17:12).

When God struck a jail in Philippi with an earthquake at midnight, cell doors flew open, freeing Paul and Silas and other prisoners. Believing his charges had escaped, the jailer became so alarmed that he drew his sword and prepared to kill himself (Acts 16:25–27). Only Paul's shout, "Don't harm yourself! We all are here!" (v. 28) curtailed the suicide.

Those who believe suicide is the unpardonable sin might label the Philippian jailer an unlikely, perhaps disqualified, candidate for salvation. However, he followed Paul's advice to believe in the Lord Jesus and became a member of God's eternal family (v. 34).

So, as heinous a sin as suicide is, it is not the unpardonable sin. Neither is the sin of cursing the Lord. Many Christians admit to having had a foul mouth prior to their conversion to Christ. They used not only coarse language but also profane language. They violated the commandment "You shall not misuse the name of the LORD your God" (Ex. 20:7). Nevertheless, when they turned in faith to the Lord, he forgave all their sins. He gave them not only a new life but also a new language. Now instead of profaning his name, they praise it.

But what about the belief that mistreating one's spouse is the unpardonable sin? Obviously, the mistreated spouse may find such treatment unpardonable, but who hasn't mistreated his or her spouse at one time or another, apologized to the spouse, and asked for and received divine forgiveness?

Is the unpardonable sin the sin of lying about your faith or denying your faith so others will accept you? Of course not! Peter denied his Lord three times in the presence of wicked men in order to save his skin, but after rising from the dead, the Lord forgave Peter and subsequently equipped him for outstanding leadership in the first-century church. Keep in mind that this man who had denied his Lord was the same individual who later proclaimed Christ to a multitude of Jews and drew 3,000 of them to Christ.

Those who believe the unpardonable sin is the act of partaking of the Lord's Supper ought to rethink their position. How many religious people with a tradition of partaking of the Lord's Supper when they were unregenerate eventually heard the gospel and became believers? Consider, too, that if the Lord imposed the penalty of eternal condemnation on believers who partook of the Lord's Supper unworthily, his promise that believers will never perish (John 10:28) would lack credibility.

So what is the sin that can never be forgiven? Obviously, all who die without having believed on Christ as Savior do not receive forgiveness beyond the grave. Hebrews 9:27 testifies, "Just as man is destined to die once, and after that to face judgment."

Several conditions existed when Jesus commented that "whoever blasphemes against the Holy Spirit will never be forgiven; he is guilty of an eternal sin" (Mark 3:29). First, Jesus was physically present as Israel's legitimate King. Second, Jesus had performed an indisputable miracle. Third, the Pharisees accused Jesus of performing miracles by the power of Satan.

Let's examine each of these conditions.

JESUS WAS PHYSICALLY PRESENT AS ISRAEL'S LEGITIMATE KING

The Old Testament had instructed Israel to anticipate the arrival of her messianic king and his kingdom. Psalm 24:7, 9 instruct, "Lift up your heads, O you gates; be lifted up, you ancient doors, that the King of glory may come in." The prophet Isaiah pointed the nation to a redemptive day, when the Prince of Peace would "reign on David's throne and over his kingdom" (9:7). He also called on the nation to "see, a king will reign in righteousness" (32:1). Daniel prophesied that "the God of heaven will set up a kingdom that will never be destroyed, nor will it be left to another people" (Dan. 2:44). Zechariah encouraged Israel to anticipate the coming of her King: "Rejoice greatly, O Daughter of Zion! Shout, Daughter of Jerusalem! See, your king comes to you, righteous and having salvation, gentle and riding on a donkey, on a colt, the foal of a donkey" (Zech. 9:9).

These prophecies were fulfilled in part when Jesus came to earth. As King David's most prominent descendant, he was born "king of the Jews" (Matt. 2:2) and offered himself to Israel as her King (see Matt. 21:1–5). However, the nation rejected her King and called upon Governor Pilate to crucify him. But when the governor's soldiers nailed Jesus to a cross, they placed a sign above his head that announced in Aramaic, Latin, and Greek, THE KING OF THE JEWS (Matt. 27:37; John 19:20). Offended by the designation, Israel's chef priests protested to Pilate. They demanded, "Do not write 'The King of the Jews,' but that this man claimed to be king of the Jews" (John 19:21). Obviously, they knew Jesus had presented himself to the nation as her king, but they had scorned him.

Someday, the Old Testament prophecies of a messianic king reigning over Israel—and the Gentiles too—will be fulfilled completely. Jesus will return to the Mount of Olives, smite his enemies, enter Jerusalem, and establish his government (see Zech. 14:1–5, 16–17; Acts 1:11–12; Rev. 19:11–16).

The gospel of Matthew, written to present Jesus to Israel as her rightful King, teems with references to the "king" and "kingdom." We should not be surprised to find Jesus speaking about the kingdom and the unpardonable sin in close proximity in Matthew 12:25–32. (See appendix E. I believe, in fact, that neither King Jesus nor the kingdom God promised to Israel is present today on earth.)

Jesus had performed an indisputable miracle

Examining the context in which Jesus spoke about the unpardonable sin, we learn that he had healed a demon-possessed man (Matt. 12:22). The event was one of many miracles he performed in the power of the Holy Spirit as evidence that he was Israel's Messiah. The apostle Peter testified that "God anointed Jesus of Nazareth with the Holy Spirit and power, and … he went around doing good and healing all who were under the power of the devil, because God was with him" (Acts 10:38).

Jesus was conceived of the Holy Spirit (Luke 1:35), anointed by the Holy Spirit (3:21–22; 4:18–21), and filled with the Holy Spirit (4:1, 14). Israel should have recognized by Jesus' miracles that he was her messianic king. The apostle John, a Jew, constructed the gospel of John around eight of Jesus' miracles to prove that Jesus was the Christ (the Messiah) and to incite saving faith in him. He wrote in 20:30–31, "Jesus did many other miraculous signs in the presence of his disciples, which are not recorded in this book. But these are written that you may believe that Jesus is the Christ, the Son of God, and that by believing you may have life in his name."

You may recall that God promised Israel many centuries before Jesus was born that he would raise up a prophet like Moses (Deut. 18:15, 18). He said that he would put his words in that prophet's mouth and that the prophet would tell the people everything he would command him. God included a warning with this prophecy: "If anyone does not listen to my words that the prophet speaks in my name, I myself will call him to account" (v. 19).

Think back to the burning bush event. God spoke to Moses from the midst of a burning bush in Midian and commissioned him to redeem the Hebrew slaves from Egypt. With the commission came the supernatural power to perform signs and wonders not only to persuade Pharaoh to release the Hebrews but also to convince the Hebrews that Moses was God's authentic prophet and deliverer.

Centuries later Jesus arrived in Israel as God's anointed prophet who declared God's words and brought redemption to the nation. His miracles clearly validated his credentials. Some members of the nation believed when they heard his words and observed his miracles, but the nation as a whole rejected his teachings, his miracles, and his deliverance. The nation's leaders were especially adamant in their rejection of Jesus.

The apostle Paul, who had risen to the top of Jewish ranks because of his knowledge and zeal for Mosaic law and the traditions of the Jews, wrote that the "Jews demand miraculous signs" (1 Cor. 1:22). Interestingly, after Jesus pronounced the eternal sentence that accompanies the unpardonable sin, some Pharisees and teachers of the law said to him, "Teacher, we want to see a miraculous sign from you" (Matt. 12:38). Had they not already seen Jesus perform miraculous signs? How many more would it take to convince them that he was the Messiah? Obviously even miracles in profusion would not soften their stony hearts!

So the unpardonable sin involved the physical presence of Jesus on earth, presenting himself as Israel's King and performing indisputable miracles. These conditions do not exist today.

THE PHARISEES ACCUSED JESUS OF PERFORMING MIRACLES BY THE POWER OF SATAN

As we have seen, Jesus performed miracles by the power of the Holy Spirit. The eyewitnesses to Jesus' miracle of the exorcising demons from a blind mute (Matt. 12:22; Luke 11:14) did not dispute this fact. As a matter of fact, they were so astonished that they entertained the thought that Jesus was the Messiah. "Could this be the Son of David?" they asked (Matt. 12:23). This miracle, like all the others Jesus performed, clearly testified that Jesus was indeed Israel's Messiah.

However, upon hearing the eyewitnesses' question, the Pharisees countered that Beelzebub, the prince of demons, had possessed Jesus and empowered him to drive out demons (Matt. 12:24; Mark 3:22).

Beelzebub, the Greek form of the Hebrew name Baal-Zebub, meaning *lord of the flies*, was commonly used in ancient times as a synonym for Satan, the Devil. The Pharisees were attributing the work of the Holy Spirit to Satan and therefore were guilty of the sin of blasphemy against the Holy Spirit (Matt. 12:31). The Spirit had testified by Jesus' miracles that the Messiah and his kingdom had arrived (Matt. 12:28; Luke 11:20), but the Pharisees had rejected both. By doing so, they jeopardized their eternal destiny. Jesus warned, "Anyone who speaks against the Holy Spirit will not be forgiven, either in this age or in the age to come" (Matt. 12:32).

Having placed the warning about the unpardonable sin in its biblical context, we can see that it related to Israel when her messianic king was on earth, offering his kingdom and validating his royal credentials by performing miracles in the power of the Holy Spirit. This sin cannot be committed today.

Nevertheless, a sin persists today that cannot be forgiven. It is the sin of rejecting Jesus Christ as Savior. The invitation to believe in Jesus as Savior and receive the gift of eternal life extends to all who have fallen short of

God's standard of righteousness (Matt. 11:28; Acts 16:31; Rom. 6:23; 10:13), but death stamps "Canceled" on the invitation.

A dying thief received the gift of eternal life by believing in Jesus. Saul of Tarsus, an accomplice to Stephen's murder, a persecutor of believers, and an enemy of Christ, received eternal life when he believed in Jesus. Some of the Corinthians had been sexually immoral, idolaters, adulterers, male prostitutes, homosexual offenders, thieves, greedy persons, drunkards, slanderers, or swindlers, but they received a new and eternal life by believing in Jesus (1 Cor. 6:9–11, 19–20). So there is hope this side of the grave for the worst of sinners to become the best of saints. No one should think he or she cannot be forgiven. God's grace avails to forgive any sin and all sins.

Frequently a funeral service includes the playing of "Amazing Grace" by a bagpiper. Occasionally, it is sung at funerals. John Newton, the writer of this beloved gospel song, had been a slave trader. One day, however, John faced the ugliness of his sin and turned in faith to Jesus Christ for forgiveness and a brand-new life. "Amazing Grace" expresses his gratitude for the grace God bestowed on him by granting forgiveness and a new life. It begins, "Amazing grace!—how sweet the sound—That saved a wretch like me." That amazing grace is available until death.

Beware the Unpardonable Sin!

At the close of a worship service, a church member commented to her new pastor, "Pastor, I have been of this church for more than forty years, but I never knew what sin was until you became our pastor." Hopefully, if she reads this chapter, she will even know what the unpardonable sin is.

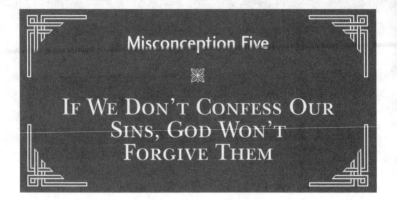

I f confession is good for the soul, why was a dusty confessional offered on eBay to the highest bidder? A
church in Vienna, Austria, placed the cherry-wood confessional in auction as a last resort to get rid of it and
commented that the congregation planned to give it away
if it didn't sell. The church must have had another confessional in use, because the one listed on eBay was
gathering dust in a storage room. (I'm not sure if the confessional ever sold or not.)

Of course, a Christian doesn't need a confessional to
confess his or her sins to the Lord. God is available to hear
a confession whenever and wherever a believer offers it.
Furthermore, he will respond to sincere confession with
forgiveness and cleansing. First John 1:9 promises, "If we
confess our sins, he is faithful and just and will forgive us
our sins and purify us from all unrighteousness."

Some students of the Bible might argue that 1 John 1:9
applies to unbelievers. They see the verse as an invitation

to unbelievers to confess their sins and receive cleansing. However, unbelievers might readily admit they are sinful, confess every sin filed in their memory bank, and still not receive cleansing. Personal salvation cannot be acquired by confessing sin, but by confessing the Lord Jesus and believing in your heart that God has raised him from the dead (Rom. 10:9–10). God gives salvation by grace through faith, "not by works" (Eph. 2:8–9).

A glance at the context in which the apostle John wrote 1 John 1:9 reveals that this verse applies to Christians. His frequent use of "we" (ten times) and "us" (four times) in verses 6 to 10 indicates that he was addressing members of God's family. Like a caring, elderly father, John arranged his first letter as though he were conducting a family talk. He often addressed his readers as "dear children" (2:1, 12–13, 18, 28; 3:7, 18; 4:4; 5:21) and "dear friends" (2:7; 3:21; 4:1, 7). This is the language of love written to children of the loving heavenly Father.

But even in families guided by a loving father, children push beyond the limits of their father's house rules. I never doubted that my father loved me, although I wasn't always thrilled with some of his rules. When I broke a rule, I did not cease being Dad's son, but I endangered our relationship. I learned that it was better to admit a transgression, "face the music," and receive forgiveness than to cover it up and feel miserable—unable to look Dad in the eye.

When I became a Christian at age sixteen, I quickly discovered that my heavenly Father, too, had family rules: no lying, no stealing, no impure thinking, no selfish behavior, love God, love your neighbor as yourself, be honest, work hard, live above reproach, etc. I learned that he did not disown me when I broke a rule, but I felt miserable when I did. Sin disturbed the fellowship that existed between my heavenly Father and me. Like a wall that had gone up between us, it needed to come down. Fortunately, confession prepared the way for God's forgiveness to crush the wall and build renewed fellowship in its place.

It is this fellowship between a believer and the Father in heaven that the apostle John wrote about. He explained that we cannot enjoy fellowship with God while we "walk in the darkness" (1 John 1:6). Fellowship with God is conditional. We must "walk in the light, as he is in the light" (v. 7). As long as we walk in the light, "we have fellowship with one another" (v. 7); that is, we have fellowship with our Father, and he has fellowship with us. When we sin, we lose that fellowship until we confess the sin.

In my college days I met many sincere Christian students who believed that God would cast them into hell if they failed to confess their sins. They equated unconfessed sins with loss of salvation. So they tried at day's end to recall every sin they had committed and then confess it before nodding off to sleep.

One day, three students and I were driving from New York State to Virginia and singing hymns as we motored down Highway 15. (Yes, we sang hymns!) I was the only student in the car who believed that every believer possesses irrevocable eternal life. The others believed they would lose eternal life if they failed to stay 'fessed up.

After singing a rousing couple of stanzas of "Blessed Assurance," I asked my friends how blessed or assuring their salvation was if they failed to confess all their sins. "What would happen if you lost your lives in a car crash on this trip and missed your nightly routine of confessing your sins?"

Only the purr of new tires invaded the ensuing silence.

Frankly, I don't think any Christian can maintain an accurate mental or written daily record of his or her sins. Even a Christian addicted to a Palm Pilot would fail to note some sins. (And isn't it a sin to be addicted to an electronic device?) Our sins fall into two broad categories: sins of commission (we do what we should not do) and sins of omission (we fail to do what we should do). The apostle Paul admitted: "I do not understand what I do. For what I want to do I do not do, but what I hate I do" (Rom. 7:15). Expanding on this enigma, he wrote, "For I have the desire to do what is good, but I cannot carry it out. For what I do is not the good I want to do; no, the evil I do not want to do—this I keep on doing" (vv. 18–19).

You and I have stood in Paul's sandals, haven't we?

If staying saved depended upon confessing every sin, we would never stay saved. Even if we could account for every wrong we did and confess it, we could not possibly keep track of everything we should have done but failed to do. And lest we think the latter offenses are not sins, James 4:17 charges: "Anyone, then, who knows the good he ought to do and doesn't do it, sins."

In Old Testament times, God required sacrifices for sins of omission. Obviously, he did not dismiss such matters as inconsequential. Leviticus 5:17–18 states: "If a person sins and does what is forbidden in any of the LORD's commands, even though he does not know it, he is guilty and will be held responsible. He is to bring to the priest as a guilt offering a ram from the flock, one without defect and of the proper value. In this way the priest will make atonement for him for the wrong he has committed unintentionally, and he will be forgiven."

What a relief to find that the context for 1 John 1:9 involves fellowship between a believer and the heavenly Father and not instructions for receiving or retaining salvation. But why does a child of God need the forgiveness and cleansing identified in 1 John 1:9? Didn't every child of God receive forgiveness in Christ when he or she became a believer? The answer is yes.

Ephesians 1:7 assures us that in Christ "we have redemption through his blood, the forgiveness of sins, in accordance with the riches of God's grace." But this perspective relates to the justification we each have because we are seated with Christ in the heavenlies (2:6). We are also glorified in Christ (Rom. 8:30), but we don't always live in a Christlike manner. Our standing in Christ never changes. In him, we are fully forgiven, completely justified, entirely sanctified, and thoroughly glorified. Our state, however, may vary like a swirling wind. One moment, we honor our heavenly Father by doing his will. The next moment, we dishonor him by sinning.

As we have seen, we do not lose salvation when we sin, but we disrupt our fellowship with our heavenly Father. In order to restore that fellowship, we must confess our sins.

In his model prayer, Jesus taught us to pray to our Father in heaven and, among other things, beseech him to "forgive us our sins" (Luke 11:4). Obviously, then, born-again men and women need daily forgiveness.

But what did the apostle John mean by "confess" in 1 John 1:9? The word "confess" in this verse is *homologomen*, meaning "acknowledge, agree, say the same thing." We ought to acknowledge our sins, agree with our Father that our sins are offensive, and assume his attitude toward sin. He sees sin as ugly, unholy, vile, and villainous. His Son Jesus bore the weight of our sins on the cross, became sin for us, and paid the utmost penalty for our sins. Our sins, therefore, are not simply minor infractions but heinous crimes against God. They are characteristic of "darkness" (1 John 1:6), and by acknowledging this fact and adopting God's perspective about sin, we escape the darkness and flee to the "light." Our Father forgives us and purifies (cleanses) us from all unrighteousness (v. 9).

Can you recall how comforting it was to receive forgiveness from your earthly father after admitting that you had done wrong? When he forgave you and wrapped his arms around you, you felt secure in his love and at peace with him. Similarly, confession of sin brings a sense of well-being to the soul. We sense God's arms of love enfolding us while his peace settles upon our soul. Fellowship is sweet once again!

Perhaps an incident from Jesus' fellowship with his disciples will help us grasp the difference between the cleansing from sin that occurs at salvation and the cleansing that occurs when we confess our sins.

Jesus and his disciples assembled in an upper room, where he would instruct his men about his imminent death and its implications for them. Normally, a household slave would refresh houseguests by washing their feet, but no slave was present. Jesus, therefore, assumed the role. He "got up from the meal, took off his outer clothing, and wrapped a towel around his waist. After that, he poured water into a basin and began to wash his disciples' feet, drying them with the towel that was wrapped around him" (John 13:4–5). When Peter saw that Jesus was about to wash his feet, he remonstrated. "No," he said, "you shall never wash my feet" (v. 8).

"Unless I wash you, you have no part with me," Jesus replied.

Peter got the message. He responded, "Then, Lord, … not just my feet but my hands and my head as well!" (v. 9).

Jesus turned down this request, saying, "A person who has had a bath needs only to wash his feet; his whole body is clean" (v. 10).

What was going on? By faith in Jesus, Peter had already received a "bath"—a complete washing from sin. Having had that "bath," he did not need to be cleansed from sin all over again. However, as he walked through an unclean world, he became defiled by sins and needed partial cleansing.

The foot-washing imagery comes from first-century Roman culture. The Romans frequented public baths, where they washed thoroughly. But as they walked home, dirt from the dusty roads adhered to their feet. Upon seeing dust on their feet, they would not return to the public bath for another full washing; they would simply wash their feet or have a servant perform the washing. Similarly, once a person has been cleansed from all sin and has been justified in God's sight, he doesn't have to be fully cleansed again. He has received complete forgiveness. But as he walks through life, he picks up some of the dust (defilement) of a sinful world and needs to have only "his feet washed." Confession obtains the partial cleansing.

As a boy living only four miles from Lake Ontario, I often frequented the Port Dalhousie beach and swam in the lake. The hot, slightly tan sand felt great, and the lake water was refreshing. However, after walking from the water to my towel and belongings, I was keenly aware of sand scrunched between my toes and sticking to my feet. What was I to do to get rid of it? I had two options. The first was totally unacceptable. I could swim in the lake again. A swim would definitely wash the sand from my feet. But how could I return to my towel and belongings again with clean feet? The other option made sense. I could fill a small bucket with water and pour it over my sandy feet. Yes, a partial washing would work just fine!

I have often thought of the lake-sand experience as illustrative of the full cleansing received at conversion and the partial cleansing received through confession. Titus 3:5 refers to the "washing of rebirth," and 1 John 1:9 refers to the cleansing of confession.

Failure to confess our sins does lead to unhappy consequences that the Holy Spirit wants to help us avoid. For this reason, Ephesians 4:30 counsels, "And do not grieve the Holy Spirit of God, with whom you were sealed for the day of redemption."

Unconfessed sin injures our prayers. The psalmist who penned Psalm 66 admitted, "If I had cherished sin in my heart, the Lord would not have listened" (v. 18). Just as logs might jam a river and have to be removed before the water can flow freely, so sins can jam the prayer line to God until he removes them when we confess them.

Occasionally the efforts of concerned fellow believers are required to restore a sinning Christian. Galatians 6:1 urges "spiritual" believers to "restore" a brother who "is caught in a sin." The Greek word for "restore" was commonly used to mean the setting of bones. A dislocated arm, for example, would need to be restored. Left alone, it would cause pain and be useless.

Learning to ride a bicycle seemed to be a painfully slow process when I was a boy. My impatience spurred me to find a shortcut to acquire the skill. Convinced that it was easier to balance my bike at a fast speed than at a slow speed, I took it to the top of a hill, climbed on, and pushed off. Almost instantly I was speeding downhill, hands on the handlebars but feet off the pedals. About halfway down the hill I lost control and crashed into a curb. I flew over the handlebars and stretched out my left arm to brace my fall. It was not a good plan, but it was my only plan. Sprawled facefirst on the ground, I saw my left arm jackknife at the elbow. I had dislocated my arm.

~ 65 ~

I picked up my bicycle with my right arm and walked it home. I wondered how my parents would respond when I explained what had happened. *They can't afford a doctor's bill or a hospital bill,* I told myself. But I knew something had to be done. A dislocated arm would render me useless in my favorite sports—hockey and golf—and keep me from doing many everyday tasks. Besides, I wanted the pain to stop as soon as possible.

My parents didn't lecture me. Instead, they rushed me to the hospital, where a doctor reset the bones and placed my arm in a sling. Gradually the pain subsided, and I was able to play hockey and golf again.

A sinning Christian who fails to confess his sin is like a dislocated arm. He hurts, and he is unable to serve the Lord effectively. He may need caring fellow believers to come alongside him, counsel him, and persuade him to confess the error of his way. Then, when he is restored, he can enjoy the peace and productivity that accompany renewed fellowship with the Father.

Colorado is a health-conscious state, and its sunny, dry climate seems to contribute to the jogging's popularity. On almost any given day, joggers take to the streets, trails, paths, and roads for a good workout. I am not one of them, although I walk every day. I have noticed, though, that joggers wear very light clothes. Running shoes, athletic socks, shorts, T-shirts, and a cap make up their attire. I have never seen a jogger with combat boots, heavy pants, an overcoat, a thick scarf, and a fur hat. Jogging while wearing heavy clothes makes about as much sense as fighting a five-alarm fire with a toy water pistol. Yet, some believers try to run the Christian race with a heavy weight of sin in their lives.

Hebrews 12:1 encourages us to "throw off everything that hinders and the sin that so easily entangles, and let us run with perseverance the race marked out for us." Confession is a good way to get rid of excess baggage, so we can run well.

On your mark! Ready! Set! Go!

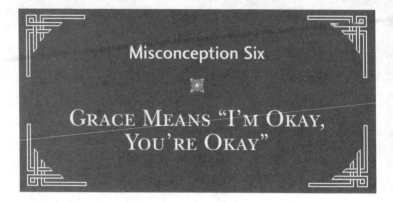

Solid Rock Church boasts that it has the best church constitution and bylaws in Springfield County, and according to its pastor they are almost as binding on the membership as the Bible itself. He especially likes the Church Covenant section that includes such statements as "We, the members of Solid Rock Church, agree to refrain from all worldly habits. We will abstain from the use of alcohol, tobacco, and the recreational use of drugs. We further agree that we will not dance, gamble, or view secular movies. We will dress modestly at all times and conduct ourselves in a manner befitting New Testament Christians."

Grace House, just five blocks from Solid Rock, organized as a church two years ago, but already its attendance has skyrocketed to eight hundred. Although it offers three Sunday morning services and a Saturday night service, it has become obvious that the congregation needs a much bigger building.

If you were to ask almost anyone who attends Grace House what he or she finds so attractive, you would most likely hear, "I have found the grace teaching so liberating. No one on the staff tells me it's wrong to do this or that."

Unlike Solid Rock Church, Grace House doesn't have a church covenant. Nor does it have a membership. The pastoral staff and a board of elders map the church's direction and oversee a ministry of small care groups.

These contrasting philosophies of Christian living are fairly typical of two categories of churches, although some churches don't belong in either one. The Solid Rock category would call churches in the Grace House category worldly. The Grace House category would call churches in the Solid Rock category legalistic. Solid Rock–type churches allege that Grace House churches teach cheap grace and insist that grace doesn't give any Christian a license to live like a pagan. Grace House–type churches argue that legalism enslaves its adherents and burdens them with heavy baggage and a guilty conscience. According to Grace House and other churches like it, if the Bible doesn't specifically mention a behavior, believers are free to pursue it. A Christian should not judge his fellow Christian. Rather his attitude should be "I'm okay, you're okay."

This issue of legalism versus the I'm-okay-you're-okay philosophy stretches all the way back to the first century and comes under scrutiny in several of the apostle Paul's

New Testament letters. But before we see how Paul addressed this issue, let's understand that in the strictest sense of the word legalism is a system of religion that depends on the keeping of rules or laws for salvation. However, in the popular sense it identifies a rigid Christian lifestyle in which a person's spirituality is judged by what he or she does or does not do. We must also understand that teaching grace is a biblical mandate. We must teach salvation by grace and encourage one another to rely on God's grace for victory over temptation, trials, and sin. But we must not cheapen grace by teaching that grace allows us to live without regard for our personal testimony. After all, God summons all his children to live righteously and godly.

In the days of Moses, God instructed the Israelites: "Consecrate yourselves and be holy, because I am the LORD your God" (Lev. 20:7). Centuries later, the apostle Peter delivered a similar divine summons—this time to Christians: "But just as he who called you is holy, so be holy in all you do; for it is written: 'Be ye holy, because I am holy'" (1 Peter 1:15–16).

It is noteworthy that Paul linked grace and righteous living together in his letter to Titus. He explained: "For the grace of God that brings salvation has appeared to all men. It teaches us to say 'No' to ungodliness and worldly passions, and to live self-controlled, upright and godly lives in this present age" (2:11–12).

Indeed, God gave us the Bible to teach us not only how to be saved but also how to live in a manner befitting saved people. Paul explained to Timothy: "You have known the holy Scriptures, which are able to make you wise for salvation through faith in Christ Jesus. All Scripture is God-breathed and is useful for teaching, rebuking, correcting and training in righteousness" (2 Tim. 3:15–16).

Who can deny, then, that believers ought to lead righteous lives? But does the legalism produce righteous lives? Does righteous living spring from the belief that Christians are free to live independent of rules?

In Romans, chapter 14, Paul described the legalistic brother as one whose faith is weak (v. 1). Most likely he was a Jew who believed in Jesus as the Messiah, but he carried into the Christian life a number of dietary restrictions and the observance of the Sabbath and other special days. Feeling obligated to keep the Mosaic law, the weak brother differed with his brothers and sisters in Christ in matters of conscience. He had not yet perceived that Jesus Christ had fulfilled the law and freed believers from its curse. Earlier in his letter to the Romans, Paul had written: "Therefore, there is now no condemnation for those who are in Christ Jesus, because through Christ Jesus the law of the Spirit of life set me free from the law of sin and death" (8:1–2). He called upon the church at Rome to accept the weak believer.

Ironically, legalistic Christians generally think they are strong in the faith and others are weak. When I was a young pastor, I served a church that had a rule for almost everything. Although many of its members possessed tons of Bible facts, some were intolerant of Christians whom they considered "unspiritual." The judgmental church members refused to take a Sunday newspaper, take a leisurely Sunday drive, eat out on Sunday, or work on Sunday. They seemed to calculate their spirituality by the number of prohibitions they observed. Their legalistic attitude kept me on my toes and on my knees. I had to spend a great amount of time putting out fires ignited by caustic attitudes and scorching remarks.

One day, I led a mother, a father, and their teenage daughter to Christ. The family had never heard the good news of salvation and expressed great joy upon learning that forgiveness is a gift. They started attending our church and seemed pleased to discover that I preached, as they remarked, "straight from the Bible."

To show that he appreciated his new Christian family, Tad, the father, mowed the church's lawn one Sunday afternoon. But his act of appreciation caught the eye of a gnarly and snarly deacon. Alarmed by this "violation" of the Lord's Day, the deacon called the church's board together that evening and suggested I pay Tad a visit. My instructions were: "Tell Tad he dishonored the Lord's Day and weakened the testimony of our church."

I replied, "Tad mowed the lawn as an act of appreciation and love. How can we censure an act like that?"

Later, I thanked Tad for mowing the lawn. If I had read the law of the Medes and the Deacons to him, I believe he would have been confused and reluctant to do anything else for the church. Fortunately, the incident passed, and Tad and his wife and their daughter became active church members, whose vibrant, young faith infused uncommon joy into our congregation.

Paul's letter to the Galatian churches sounds an alarm about legalism. The Galatian believers had stepped out of paganism to embrace new life in Christ. But along came religious teachers who told them they could not be acceptable to God unless they received the Jewish rite of circumcision and agreed to keep the Mosaic law. Like so many religious teachers before and after them, these "Judaizers" believed God rewards religious deeds by saving those who perform them. Paul exposed the error of this belief by telling the Galatians they were not obligated to keep the law. The law's purpose, he explained, was to reveal sin and the need of a Savior. He pointed out that Jesus fulfilled the law, paid our penalty by dying on the cross, and justified all who believe in him (see Gal. 2:15–16; 3:10–13, 19–23).

Legalistic attitudes destroy congregational unity. The legalists establish false standards of righteousness and criticize those who choose not to adopt those standards. ~~They backbite and condemn~~ others while showcasing their loyalty to rules. Like the Pharisees branded as hypocrites, they find little faults in others but ignore their own faults. The question Jesus asked the Pharisees is appropriate to ask legalists today: "Why do you look at the speck of sawdust in your brother's eye and pay no attention to the plank in your own eye?" (Matt. 7:3).

Both in Galatians and in Philippians the apostle Paul alluded to the divisive, destructive nature of legalism. Having urged the Galatians to stand firm in Christian liberty and reject legalism (5:1–12), he warned: "If you keep on biting and devouring each other, watch out or you will be destroyed by each other" (v. 15). In Philippians 3:2, he counseled: "Watch out for those dogs, those men who do evil, those mutilators of the flesh." Then he renounced all the legalistic trappings of the preconversion life he led as a strict Pharisee. Every religious credential and code of conduct he thought earned him favor with God, he had cast aside when he trusted in Christ alone to save him (vv. 4–9).

Although the Philippian church had maintained a strong partnership with Paul in spreading the gospel (1:3–5), it faced a crisis. Two female workers in the church, Euodia and Syntyche, had squared off in a bitter dispute (4:2). They needed to reconcile and get back on track (v. 3); otherwise, their personal feud might split the congregation into warring factions.

Perhaps these women favored opposite viewpoints, one favoring legalism and the other the free-to-do-as-I-please view. The latter view received Paul's indictment in 3:18–19: "Many live as enemies of the cross of Christ. Their destiny is destruction, their god is their stomach, and their glory is in their shame. Their mind is on earthly things."

I subscribe to the theory that a legalist may be guilty of the very things he condemns. For example, the person who carps constantly against the evil of pornography may secretly entertain sexual lusts.

Summer camp ought to provide fun and opportunity for spiritual growth for kids, but a legalistic pastor almost drained both from a camp for nine- to eleven-year-old kids. As a fellow pastor and camp teacher, I was appalled by the legalistic pastor's comments. "Some of the girls are wearing pants," he began. "We need to call their parents and advise them to bring dresses for their daughters to change into. We cannot permit girls to wear pants. It is immodest apparel."

Several months later, the front page of our local newspaper carried the shocking story that the legalistic pastor had been arrested for placing obscene phone calls to women in the community, including some in his congregation.

Legalism didn't work for a youth pastor either. He insisted that the teenage boys in his church maintain short haircuts. Hair below the ears was a no-no. So were blue jeans, which he insisted were a sign of rebellion. However, green jeans were okay. The teenage girls were prohibited from wearing pants, and their skirts and dresses had to reach below their knees. He lectured on the evils of movies and railed against rock music. His "ministry" ended when someone recognized him in a XXX-rated movie theater and reported him to the senior pastor.

My wife encountered legalism up close and personal when a female neighbor visited her on our front porch. My wife was wearing pants, and the neighbor accused her of indecency. "How come you're a pastor's wife and you're wearing pants?" she asked in a caustic tone.

My wife took the criticism graciously, but she could have asked the critic: "How come you profess to be a Christian but lock your young children out of the house all day? How come you stick your head outdoors occasionally and swear at your children to be quiet?"

As Jesus indicated, legalists seem more concerned about the speck of sawdust in another person's eye than the plank in their own eye.

But I'm-okay-you're-okay Christians don't find anything in anyone's eye, including their own. Unless the Bible specifically calls an activity sin, they are free to do whatever they want and extend the same license to their Christian brothers and sisters. "Isn't that what grace is all about?" they ask. Who can say a Christian shouldn't down a cocktail or two at the office party or play poker or participate in a football pool or invest a few dollars in the lottery or play the ponies or the puppies or smoke pot occasionally or attend R- or X-rated movies or party the night away?

If we had to produce specific verses of Scripture mentioning and prohibiting those activities, we would face a hopeless task. Not even an exhaustive concordance uncovers the word "cocktail" in the Bible. Nor does the Bible mention poker, the lottery, pot smoking, football pools, R-rated movies (or any movies), partying, or many other activities legalists label unholy.

But grace does not issue believers a license to sin. We are free from sin, but we are not free to sin. Romans 6:1–2 reasons: "What shall we say, then? Shall we go on sinning so that grace may increase? By no means! We died to sin; how can we live in it any longer?" Grace has made us free to "live a new life" (v. 4). We have been saved by grace (Eph. 2:8–9) in order to "do good works, which God prepared in advance for us to do" (v. 10).

Legalists ought to make an attitude adjustment and recognize that righteous living is not the product of the flesh. No matter how hard a Christian tries to produce righteous characteristics, he will fail, because righteous character is produced by the Holy Spirit, not manufactured by the human will. "The fruit of the Spirit is love, joy, peace, patience kindness, goodness, faithfulness, gentleness and self-control. Against such things there is no law" (Gal. 5:22–23).

Those who think grace allows them to live as they please need to adjust their attitude and recognize that the fruitful Christian life includes the quality "self-control." Self-indulgence, on the other hand, militates against the Spirit's efforts to produce godly character.

So how can a Christian decide whether an activity is right or wrong if the Bible doesn't mention it? Here are a few guidelines.

DECIDE WHETHER PARTICIPATING IN THE ACTIVITY WILL ADVANCE OR RETARD YOUR SPIRITUAL GROWTH

The main goal of the Christian life is to do the will of God (see Rom. 12:1–2). We ought to consider harmful any activity that keeps us from fulfilling God's plan for us. The activity may consume too much time that belongs to God. It may become an obsession. It may lead to a similar but clearly immoral activity. For example, a believer may feel that he can view R-rated movies without being affected negatively by the foul language and vile images. He may say, "I can chew what's good and spit out the rest," but eventually he may spit out practically nothing. Having become affected by wrong thinking, he may engage in wrong living. Garbage in, garbage out is a biblical principle. No wonder Philippians 4:8 admonishes us to think noble and pure thoughts.

The apostle John urged his readers to cast off harmful cravings and lusts, knowing that "the world and its desires pass away, but the man who does the will of God lives forever" (1 John 2:17).

A billionaire who had advertised for a chauffeur gave each applicant a road test in the rugged mountains near his mansion. He instructed each applicant to drive up the steepest road to dizzying heights. After reaching an extremely high point where there were no guardrails, he asked each applicant to drive as close to the edge of a steep cliff as possible.

One applicant drove within a foot of the drop-off. Another drove within six inches. The third drove within an inch of the cliff's edge. The fourth stayed on course; he did not even try to drive close to the edge.

The billionaire hired the fourth chauffeur, explaining that he had simply tested the applicants to see which one would resist the urge to see how close to the edge he could get without going over it. He felt safe with the one who showed no interest in seeing how close he could get to the edge without falling off.

The world offers thrills as it beckons Christians to live on the edge, but wise Christians refuse to risk the danger that lies in heeding its call.

DECIDE WHETHER PARTICIPATING IN THE ACTIVITY WILL ENHANCE OR HURT GOD'S REPUTATION

To a great extent your non-Christian friends, associates, and neighbors build their concept of God on the basis of what they see you do. If you refrain from evil conversation and evil conduct, they will most likely perceive God as righteous. If you display a careless attitude toward sin, they will most likely perceive God as unrighteous or amoral.

Jesus instructed his followers to "let your light shine before men, that they may see your good deeds and praise your Father in heaven" (Matt. 5:16).

Paul counseled, "So whether you eat or drink or whatever you do, do it all for the glory of God" (1 Cor. 10:31), and he challenged the Christians at Philippi to "shine like stars in the universe" (Phil. 2:15).

Who hasn't walked in the open on a clear night, gazed at the stars, marveled at their brilliance, and reflected on the glory of the Creator? When clouds cover the night sky, though, they hide the stars from our view, and we are less likely to think about the Creator's glory. Like a dense cloud cover, activities that fall into a gray area may dim our light and veil God's glory.

DECIDE WHETHER PARTICIPATING IN THE ACTIVITY WILL CAUSE A WEAKER BELIEVER TO STUMBLE

As we have seen, in his letter to the Romans. Paul identified the Christian with legalistic attitudes as "him whose faith is weak" (14:1). But a Christian whose faith is strong must consider how participating in a questionable activity might affect his weak brother or sister. Paul advised, "It is better not to eat meat or drink wine or to do anything else that will cause your brother to fall" (v. 21).

The Christian life is the liberated life. Christ has set us free (John 8:36), but our liberty must be balanced by love. If we love God, we will keep his commandments and refuse to do anything that dishonors him. If we love our fellow Christian, we will try to build him up in the faith and refuse to do anything that might offend his conscience. Our attitude should reflect such love that we can truly say, "If what I eat *or do* causes my brother to fall into sin, I will never eat meat *or participate in that activity* again, so that I will not cause him to fall" (1 Cor. 8:13, words in italics added).

On the surface, the I'm-okay-you're-okay philosophy seems charitable, but does it lock us into a false comfort zone and keep us from becoming all that God wants us to be? If we appear to share the same likes, interests, and desires as our pagan neighbors, why should they believe we have been saved from our sins and vested with a power to live above temptation?

The biggest question of all is this: Is our lifestyle okay with God?

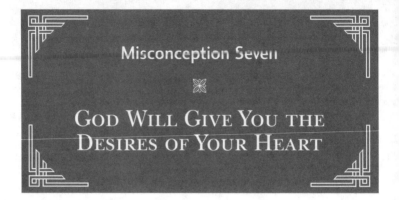

When I was a kid, the story of Aladdin and his lamp fascinated me. You remember how the lamp worked, don't you? Aladdin would simply rub the lamp and make a wish, and then, *presto*, a genie appeared to grant it. I knew the story was make-believe, but I kept my eye peeled for lamps just in case.

Several years later I became a Christian and learned that having the best things in life had nothing to do with a magic lamp but everything to do with trusting the Lord and honoring him. This understanding came about partly because I read Psalm 37:3–4:

> Trust in the LORD and do good; dwell in the land and enjoy safe pasture. Delight yourself in the LORD and he will give you the desires of your heart.

These two verses include three clear commands and a magnificent promise.

※ Command 1: "Trust in the LORD" (v. 3).

- ✼ Command 2: "and do good" (v. 3).
- ✼ Command 3: "Delight yourself in the LORD" (v. 4).
- ✼ Promise: "and he will give you the desires of your heart" (v. 4).

Think of Psalm 37:3–4 as a contractual agreement. When a buyer signs a financial agreement to purchase a car, he agrees with the seller to provide the seller with a stated down payment and pay a fixed number of monthly payments. In return, the seller agrees to provide the car the buyer has chosen.

What chance of success would you predict for a customer who selected a car from the dealer's showroom, told a salesperson that it was his heart's desire to own the car he selected, and requested it as a freebie? Nil to zilch chance of getting it? Why then would anyone think God would respond like the genie of Aladdin's lamp to grant whatever the petitioner desired?

Let's bring this issue down to a few more plausible situations.

Tavia has her heart set on owning a brand-new Victorian-style house that she can furnish with antique furniture and accents. She visualizes herself in the home of her dreams and with great pride entertaining guests. She can almost hear the guests' "oohs" and "aahs" as she guides them through the house and points out this and that authentic Victorian feature. Having read Psalm 37:4,

~ 83 ~

Tavia is convinced that God will give her the dream house fully furnished. It is, after all, one of the desires of her heart.

Monty, a sales rep, strongly desires the position of vice president of sales for Domestic Robots, Inc. He, too, believes God has promised to give him the desires of his heart. Often, he fantasizes about the prestige, power, and wealth the position would give him. He would handle a $60 million annual budget, build an efficient sales team, formulate significant policies, travel internationally, and make key decisions binding on the company's 139 sales reps. He pictures the shiny brass nameplate on the door of his spacious office and sighs at the prospect of leaving a dinky cubicle to the sales rep who succeeds him.

Bryant, a fifteen-year-old, was flipping through his Bible last month when he came across Psalm 37:4. *Wow!* he thought. *My super big desire is to be a rock star. How cool to arrive at a concert in a limo, sign a zillion autographs, and have everybody go crazy for my music! Whoa! I'm going to ask God to make it all happen.*

What do Tavia, Monty, and Bryant have in common? A misunderstanding of the promise that God gives the desires of the heart carte blanche. They failed to see that this promise comes wrapped in a contract. The conditions God imposes are not stringent, but they are uncompromising.

"Trust in the Lord" (Ps. 37:3) is the first condition

To trust means "to have faith in" or "to rely on." David, who wrote this psalm in his old age (v. 25), had learned to trust in the Lord and rely on him. Whether felling the giant Goliath or fleeing from King Saul or fending off the Philistines, David trusted in the Lord and learned that he rewards those who trust in him. David, therefore, encouraged the Israelites not to fret "because of evil men or be envious of those who do wrong" (v. 1). He assured them that "evil men will be cut off, but those who hope in the Lord will inherit the land" (v. 9).

The Lord had promised his people an earthly kingdom over which the Messiah would reign in righteousness. At times the prospect of inheriting the promised kingdom seemed bleak, but the Israelites should not worry or abandon hope. The Lord would keep his word.

Sometimes we twenty-first-century Christians neglect to trust the Lord. In our sophisticated thinking, we map out a plan that we believe will achieve happiness and fulfillment. And we lead such a fast-paced life that we want what we want when we want it. In our worldly wisdom and haste, we present our desires to the Lord for his endorsement. However, his thoughts are not our thoughts, neither are our ways his ways (Isa. 55:8). The Lord states,

"As the heavens are higher than the earth, so are my ways higher than your ways and my thoughts than your thoughts" (v. 9).

What a staggering revelation that God's ways and thoughts are so much higher than ours! Recently our concept of the distance between other planets and ours expanded. The Cassini probe satellite entered Saturn's ring plane June 30, 2004, after a seven-year voyage and sent remarkable photos back to Earth. Think of it, seven years were required for a fast-traveling space vehicle to reach this planet located 742.8 million miles from Earth. Yet, the vast expanse of the heavens reaches far beyond Saturn! So, if God's thoughts and ways are higher than ours as the heavens are higher than the earth, how can we possibly imagine that we know better than he what is best for us?

We may desire something we think will improve our life, but the Lord may not grant it because he knows it would harm our relationship with him. So for our good and his glory, he overrules our misguided wants.

Vera was in her fifties when I was her pastor. From childhood, arthritis had stiffened her body and racked it with pain. No one would have faulted her if she had desired a pain-free, flexible body; yet she would say, "Pastor, I'm glad the Lord allowed me to have arthritis. If I had been healthy as a young person, I might have partied and gotten into all kinds of trouble. The arthritis has kept me close to the Lord. I have to depend upon him just to move from one place in the house to another."

Of course, in heaven, Vera will experience neither pain nor disappointment. The Lord will reward her trust in him.

Abraham trusted in the Lord. The desire of his heart initially might have been to stay in beautiful, cultured Ur of the Chaldeans, where the livin' was easy. But, when God called him to leave Ur without announcing a destination, Abram trusted and departed.

Eventually, Abram became a nomad in Canaan. God had promise him the whole land and a son, but he spent most of his life without a son, and he never owned a stick of property except a burial cave. However, he did have an opportunity once to receive a huge reward from a king. The king of wicked Sodom offered it to him for his daring rescue of hostages and recovery of booty taken from Sodom by the armies of several powerful kings.

"Give me the people [the hostages] and keep the goods for yourself," the king of Sodom offered (Gen. 14:21).

This was Abram's big chance to pluck a fortune from the king's hands. But he trusted in the Lord and preferred to commit his future to him. Boldly he announced: "I have raised my hand to the LORD, God Most High, Creator of heaven and earth, and have taken an oath that I will accept nothing belonging to you, not even a thread or the thong of a sandal, so that you will never be able to say, 'I made Abram rich'" (vv. 22–23).

Talk about trust! But later, Abram seems to have had second thoughts about answering the king of Sodom so boldly. The Lord appeared to him and said, "Do not be afraid, Abram. I am your shield, your very great reward" (15:1). He would not only protect Abram, but also reward him. In other words, his desire for Abram was perfect! It surely exceeded anything Abram could have desired.

Abram asked what the Lord would give him, adding "since I remain childless" (v. 2).

The Lord promised to give him a son and innumerable descendants (vv. 4–5).

Abram believed the Lord (v. 6), but it would be years before he would see the fulfillment of the promise. Abram's wife was barren, and eventually Abram would be unable to father a child. But he trusted, waited, trusted, and waited until the Lord did the impossible. Abram and his wife became parents of a baby boy, whom they named Isaac.

Abram had trusted the Lord, and the Lord gave him the desire of his heart. However, the son of promise was also the Lord's desire because the Savior would be born centuries later through Isaac's lineage. The Lord's desire and Abram's desire fused into one.

A SECOND CONDITION TO REALIZING THE DESIRES OF YOUR HEART IS TO "DO GOOD" (PS. 37:3)

Psalm 84:11 affirms this truth: "For the LORD God is a sun and shield; the LORD bestows favor and honor; no good thing does he withhold from those whose walk is blameless."

Good things are not necessarily material things. In the Sermon on the Mount "blessings" are identified as citizenship in Jesus' kingdom, comfort, inheritance in the kingdom, spiritual satisfaction, mercy, the prospect of seeing God, being called God's sons, and having reward in heaven (Matt. 5:3–12). Indeed, as a noteworthy plaque suggests, "The best things in life are not things."

The apostle Paul and Demas were both missionaries, but Paul's unswerving goal was to do good—to fulfill God's will for his life. At the end of his life, he shivered in a Roman dungeon, where he awaited execution. He asked Mark to bring him the coat that he had left at Troas (2 Tim. 4:13). Obviously, he had few or no possessions, but neither did he have any complaints. He had served the Lord faithfully and therefore anticipated receiving a heavenly reward, "the crown of righteousness" (4:8). Demas, on the other hand, swerved from doing good—from doing God's will. Having "loved this world" (v. 10), he tossed aside the opportunity to receive a heavenly crown.

Like Paul and Demas, every Christian must choose whether to invest his or her life in doing good or spend his or her life in getting goods. The desires of the body may be met temporarily by getting goods, but the desires of the heart can be met only by doing good.

Of course, a wealthy Christian may do an enormous amount of good, but only if he values God's will more than wealth. Church history has had its share of wealthy believers who supported the Lord's work generously and used their money to open doors of opportunity to missions and evangelism. Actually, a Christian of meager means may be far more materialistic than a wealthy Christian. He may crave money and live to acquire it and end up losing the best things in life. Paul informed Timothy, "People who want to get rich fall into temptation and a trap and into many foolish and harmful desires that plunge men into ruin and destruction" (1 Tim. 6:9).

THE THIRD CONDITION WE MUST MEET BEFORE THE LORD GIVES US THE DESIRES OF OUR HEARTS IS, "DELIGHT YOURSELF IN THE LORD" (PS. 37:4)

Legitimately. We may find delight in any number of pursuits and pleasures. For example, we may delight in listening to a fine symphony orchestra or watching a fast-paced basketball game or reading a son or daughter's outstanding report card or standing atop a mountain and gazing at majestic scenery or reading a captivating novel. But our chief delight ought to be in the Lord.

When we delight in the Lord, we revel in his character and mighty works. We rejoice in who he is and what he does. Just as a person in love delights to spend time with the one he or she loves, so we cherish time spent with the Lord. Like Peter, who accompanied the Lord to the Mount of Transfiguration and beheld his radiant glory, we exclaim, "Lord, it is good for us to be here."

We cannot see the Lord today, but we can enjoy his presence and get well acquainted with him by reading his Word. Notice how the following excerpts from the book of Psalms link delight in the Lord with love for his Word:

> Blessed is the man who does not walk in the counsel of the wicked. . . . But his delight is in the law of the LORD. (Ps. 1:1–2)
>
> Your statutes are my delight. (Ps. 119:24)
>
> Your law is my delight. (Ps. 119:77, 174)

As we mediate on God's Word, the Holy Spirit uses it to teach us to disdain sin and desire to do what pleases God. We learn, for example, that God wants us to love him preeminently, to love others as ourselves, to hunger and thirst for righteousness, to pray, to put others' interests ahead of our own, to assume a servant's role, to evangelize, to worship "in spirit and in truth," to keep ourselves pure, to give thanks in everything, and to long for Jesus' return. We find ourselves praying, "I desire to do your will, O my God; your law is within my heart" (Ps. 40:8). Indeed, we find that our desires are precisely God's desires for us.

God's promise to give us the desires of our hearts (Ps. 37:4) fully agrees with his will for us. He is too wise to give us what violates his will and too loving and kind to withhold from us what complements it.

In the days of the judges, Hannah had a rough life. For one thing, she was barren. For another, her husband, Elkanah, had a second wife, Peninnah, who had given birth to sons and daughters. Elkanah loved Hannah, but society judged a woman's worth by the number of children, especially sons, she presented to her husband. So Hannah's self-esteem must have been lower than the Dead Sea. To make matters worse, Peninnah hassled Hannah year after year about her inability to bear a child. As a matter of fact, she drove Hannah to tears.

One day, during a trip to the tabernacle at Shiloh, Hannah wept bitterly and prayed earnestly in the presence of Eli, the priest. She prayed in her heart that the Lord would give her a son, and as she prayed, her lips pursed the words without making a sound.

Observing this, Eli though she was drunk. "How long will you keep on getting drunk?" he asked her. "Get rid of your wine" (1 Sam. 1:14).

Quickly, Hannah explained that she had not been drinking, but was pouring out her heart to the Lord.

"Go in peace, and may the God of Israel grant you what you have asked of him," Eli replied (v. 17).

Hannah strongly desired a son, and she believed in pouring out her heart to the Lord. Further, she was dedicated to the Lord. She had promised to give her son to the Lord "for all the days of his life" as a Nazarite (v. 11). The Lord was her delight and her Master. Would he give her the desire of her heart?

He would. His will called for a new judge for his people, and the son Hannah would bear would become that judge. At his birth, Hannah named her baby boy Samuel. He grew up at Shiloh under Eli's mentoring and later became Eli's successor. He served Israel as an outstanding judge and even anointed Israel's greatest king, David.

Hannah's desire and the Lord's will were fused together.

Another case of the human desire and the divine will fusing together involved David's son Solomon. When he became Israel's king, he received an opportunity from the Lord to request anything he desired. First Kings 3:5 reports that the Lord appeared to him during the night in a dream and said, "Ask for whatever you want me to give you."

This may seem like a genie-of-the-lamp story, but it was a real-time event early in Solomon's royal career, and he didn't squander the opportunity on selfish whims.

Recognizing that the Lord's will was paramount, he identified himself as the Lord's servant and asked for wisdom. Verses 8 and 9 record a portion of Solomon's request:

> Your servant is here among the people you have chosen, a great people, too numerous to count or number. So give your servant a discerning heart to govern your people and to distinguish between right and wrong. For who is able to govern this great people of yours?

Is it any wonder that "the Lord was pleased that Solomon had asked for this" and granted the request (vv. 10, 12)? The desires of Solomon's heart aligned perfectly with the desires of God's heart.

The word "desires" in Psalm 37:4 carries the meaning "petitions" and therefore brings to mind prayer requests. God grants the prayer requests of our hearts if they agree with his will. James 4:3 exposes the sin and futility of praying selfishly: "When you ask, you do not receive, because you ask with wrong motives, that you may spend what you get on your pleasures." Following the counsel of Psalm 37:3–4 to trust in the Lord, do good, and delight in the Lord is the sure way to keep selfish prayer requests at bay and to pray according to God's will. It is also the way to receive the desires of our hearts. First John 5:14–15 states, "This is the confidence we have in approaching God: that if we ask anything according to his will, he hears us. And if we know that he hears us—whatever we ask—we know that we have what we asked of him."

The father of a strong-willed ten-year-old boy reminded him often, "Buster, you must not always want your own way."

Buster dropped his head and seemed to be deep in thought. After a few moments, he answered, "Dad, if I choose to do the Lord's will because I want to, don't I still have my own way?"

Apparently Buster had learned an important truth about Christian living.

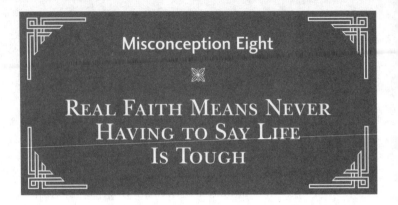

REAL FAITH MEANS NEVER HAVING TO SAY LIFE IS TOUGH

F eeling too sick to attend church, I slumped in my La-Z-Boy recliner and set the TV remote to a religious network. What I heard made me wonder if the publisher of my Bible had omitted a hundred pages. I certainly hadn't read in my copy of the Bible what that Sunday morning's TV preachers claimed.

"Jesus doesn't want you to be sick," one preacher consoled. "He died to free you from illness and disease. Today, he wants to heal you—take away the back pain or the diabetes or the migraines or the cancer or whatever else you may be suffering."

Hmmm, I reflected, *a perfectly healthy life would certainly say no to death and dying. And a couple of dollars a day donated to this preacher would work as well as an apple a day to keep the doctor away.*

Another TV preacher urged his audience to turn their finances around by planting a faith seed in his ministry. *Or was it in his pocket?*

"Aren't you tired of having unpaid bills stack up?" he asked. "Do you feel defeated because you cannot enjoy an affluent lifestyle? The apostle James hit the nail on the head. He said, 'You have not because you ask not.' And Jesus promised 'all these things' to those who seek the kingdom of God first. So I challenge you to believe and show your interest in God's kingdom by planting a faith seed of fifty or a hundred dollars in this ministry. God will return the fifty or hundred dollars to you many fold, but you have to take the first step by planting a faith seed."

Strange—the more of those TV programs I watched, the sicker I felt. But I watched one more before reaching for the Alka-Seltzer.

"I get letters from viewers who complain that their prayers aren't working," the well-dressed preacher announced. "They heard me say that God answers prayer. If you ask him specifically for a new car, a new house, or a new job, he will give it to you. These complainers forget that I said *specifically*. Let me explain.

"When I wanted the Lord to give me a Cadillac, I visited a dealer, selected a specific model, wrote down the options I wanted, and picked up a brochure with photos of the car. Then I posted the photos around the house so that I could focus on the car when I shaved, got dressed, and ate a meal. I had that car on my mind all day long, and when I prayed, I asked the Lord specifically for that

~ 97 ~

car. I told him not only the color I wanted but also the options. I was specific.

"That's how you need to pray. You haven't received what you asked for because you haven't given the Lord enough specific details!"

"Tell it to starving Christian refugees in Sudan," I found myself saying to the TV preacher. "And while you're at it, explain that the Christian life is supposed to be a bed of roses."

Most Christians realize that faith doesn't eliminate trials and open the floodgates for a deluge of years of flawless health and material prosperity. They have learned from Scripture and personal experience that faith gets us *through* each trial not *out* of it.

If you think faith is never having to say life is tough, why not review the lives of some believers in Bible times whose faith was strong? You may be surprised to learn that they suffered enormous trials.

The Bible describes Job as "blameless and upright," a man who "feared God and shunned evil" (Job 1:1). He was such a good family man that early every morning he sacrificed a burnt offering for each of his adult children (v. 5). We would have to nod our heads and affirm that Job was a man of faith. But trials began to burst like cluster bombs in Job's life.

What happened? Had Job lost his faith? Not at all. Job made two resolute declarations of faith while enduring horrendous trials. The first affirms Job's intention to keep trusting God for the rest of his life: "Though he slay me, yet will I hope in him" (13:15). The second affirms the confidence that he would see God in the afterlife: "I know that my Redeemer lives, and that in the end he will stand upon the earth. And after my skin has been destroyed, yet in my flesh I will see God; I myself will see him with my own eyes—I, and not another" (19:25–27).

Trials took away Job's livestock, his servants, his sons and daughters, and his health, but they could not take away his faith. Even when he was sitting on an ash pile and scraping pus from his sores, he trusted in the Lord as the sovereign, all-wise Creator. His wife advised Job to "curse God and die" (2:9), but Job replied, "You are talking like a foolish woman. Shall we accept good from God, and not trouble?" (v. 10).

Would you dare to suggest that Job's trials resulted from a lack of faith? I wouldn't!

Another man of faith, perhaps a contemporary of Job, learned that faith in God didn't exempt him from trials. His name was Abraham, and he had received sweeping promises from God about innumerable descendants and a vast amount of land. However, the only property Abraham ever owned was a burial plot; and he lived to light one hundred candles on his birthday cake before he and his wife, Sarah, had their first child.

~ 99 ~

Talk about trials! Abraham wandered as a stranger in a land God had promised to give him. He waited and waited and waited for the son God had promised to him. When the son, Isaac, was born, Abraham rejoiced, but joy must have dissipated when Isaac was a young teenager. God commanded Abraham to sacrifice Isaac as a burnt offering on Mount Moriah (Gen. 22:1–2). Not one to drag his feet when God issued a command, Abraham left for the designated mountain "early the next morning" (v. 3), taking Isaac with him.

This was Abraham's harshest trial. How could he realize the fulfillment of God's promise of innumerable descendants if Isaac were dead? The answer is that he exercised faith. Hebrews 11:17–19 fills in the picture: "By faith Abraham, when God tested him, offered Isaac as a sacrifice. He who had received the promises was about to sacrifice his one and only son, even though God had said to him, 'It is through Isaac that your offspring will be reckoned.' Abraham reasoned that God could raise the dead, and figuratively speaking, he did receive Isaac back from death."

What rock-solid faith Abraham had! He trusted so resolutely in God that he expected him to raise Isaac from the dead in order to fulfill his promise. But also, what an unspeakably tough trial Abraham faced! He expected to have to slay his only son on Mount Moriah. Surely, not even the prospect of seeing God raise Isaac from the dead could have removed the trauma he would have experienced. The tension between Abraham's faith in God and his love for the son of his old age was almost enough to make the mountain tremble.

A boulder-size lump formed in my throat and a mammoth ache struck my heart when I dropped our only son off at college two states away, knowing I wouldn't see him again for at least three months. Because a father loves his children, separation from any of them seems hard to bear. I cried when I left our daughters at their respective distant colleges, and tears welled up in my eyes when I performed our son's and daughters' weddings.

Beyond a doubt, the toughest trial of separation from our adult children occurred in January 1990 when my wife and I told them good-bye and left our home in Denver for a new ministry in Chicago. As Gloria and I drove away, we both felt the pain of separation. But the pain struck with vicious force when we were traveling on Interstate 76 about sixty miles from home. We were listening to KWBI, a Christian radio station in Denver, where our daughter Heather hosted a music-by-request morning program. We heard her say, "I would like to dedicate this next song to my parents, who are traveling to Chicago today." She had picked "I Thank God for My Family." Tears blocked my vision. "Do you want to turn around and go back to Denver?" I asked.

I knew she wanted to, and so did I, but we drove on. We were committed to God's will.

I can only imagine how Abraham felt when God tested his faith on Mount Moriah. He understood that faith and hard times are not mutually exclusive. But he endured the trial, believing that obedience to God's will must take precedence over everything else, including love for one's only son.

Genesis also profiles Joseph, a man of faith. In spite of dreadful treatment at the hands of his envious, vengeful brothers, the shock of being falsely accused of a crime, and the burden of a long jail sentence, he never lost his faith in God. When Joseph was finally reunited with his brothers, he reflected on the hardship they had inflicted on him and observed, "You intended to harm me, but God intended it for good to accomplish what is now being done, the saving of many lives" (Gen. 50:20).

Some who believe that faith is never having to say life is tough might have written Joseph's story differently. They would have plotted a straight, smooth line from Joseph's comfortable life as a teenager in Canaan to a throne in Egypt. But without the trials, Joseph would not have reached a throne with proven faith and a deep love for all his family members.

Genuine faith always makes us better, not bitter!

Let's leap nearly about 2,500 years ahead to the period called the Babylonian captivity. Judah and its capital, Jerusalem, had fallen to the Babylonians, and the king of Babylon, Nebuchadnezzar, had taken many of

Jerusalem's citizens into captivity. Daniel, a young man at the time, was one of those citizens. He suddenly found himself in Babylon and in training to serve in the king's court. Would his faith in Yahweh exempt him from trials in pagan Babylon?

The answer is a resounding no. Early in his Babylonian experience, Daniel encountered brainwashing and all attempts to erase his loyalty to Yahweh. The Babylonians even renamed him Belteshazzar in honor of one of their deities. But Daniel's faith triumphed over this trial of psychological and religious pressure.

Later, during Darius's reign, the king was persuaded by counselors, who were "gunning" for Daniel, to make a highly restrictive law. It forbade everyone from praying to any god or man except Darius for thirty days. Anyone who violated this law would be hurled into a lions' den. Of course the counselors' plot was designed to rid them of Daniel. They knew he was a man of faith who prayed daily to the God of Israel.

The evil scheme tried Daniel's faith, but it did not destroy or even weaken it. Daniel entered his home, went to his upstairs prayer room, and with windows opened toward Jerusalem, prayed as he always had (Dan. 6:10).

Finding Daniel on his knees and praying to Yahweh, his adversaries reported him to the king (vv. 11–15). Soon, Daniel was on the lions' menu (v. 16).

But the lions didn't touch their "food," ~~because God~~ had sent his angel to shut their mouths (v. 22). The penalty had been executed, but Daniel had not been executed. Astonished at God's power to rescue Daniel, King Darius decreed that everyone in his kingdom must fear and reverence Daniel's God.

The Bible doesn't disclose the identity of the angel who delivered Daniel, but it may have been the Lion of the Tribe of Judah, the preincarnate Christ, who is identified in other Old Testament passages as the angel of the Lord.

One thing is certain: God received more glory by bringing Daniel through his severe trial than by exempting him from it. Similarly, God receives more glory by bringing you through trials than by exempting you from them.

Jesus lived a perfect life. He never thought an evil thought or performed an evil deed. He was sinless, and his faith was peerless. But he encountered trials. Immediately after being baptized, he was driven into the wilderness, where he hungered for forty days. Then, in his weakened condition, he came under a battery of assaults from the Devil. Nevertheless, he declined every temptation the Devil hurled at him.

In his earthly ministry, Jesus experienced intense persecution at the hands of self-righteous, unbelieving religious leaders. At times, he had to dodge their attempts to stone him. He had no place to lay his head, owned no real estate, and claimed no personal belongings. At the end of his brief ministry, he saw his disciples desert him. Peter denied him three times, and Judas betrayed him. Jesus was arrested, tried in a kangaroo court, sentenced to die, mocked, beaten, spat upon, nailed to a cross prepared for a felon, ridiculed and insulted by onlookers, and left to die.

No one has ever suffered to the extent Jesus suffered. Our trials cannot begin to compare with the trials he endured. Yet, our trials should not take us by surprise. Jesus predicted, "In this world you will have trouble. But take heart! I have overcome the world" (John 16:33).

The apostles were men of great faith after Pentecost. They proclaimed Christ boldly, but they suffered brutal treatment at the hands of those who despised the name of Jesus. The book of Acts records that they were beaten and thrown into prison for giving evidence of their faith in Christ. Acts 12 reports that Herod beheaded the apostle James and apprehended the apostle Peter, intending to sever Peter's head from his body after Passover (vv. 1–4). But the angel of the Lord rescued Peter from prison.

Perhaps you wonder why God didn't rescue James. Why did James die, yet Peter lived? You might apply that question to contemporary life. Why does one cancer-stricken believer die, whereas another survives? Or you may ask why a particularly dedicated Christian teenager nearly dies in an auto accident and must experience long months filled with surgeries and rehabilitation, whereas less dedicated teenagers enjoy an almost carefree youth.

We may never receive satisfactory answers to such questions, but we can accept what Scripture teaches about the purpose of trials.

An Illinois pastor and his wife must have asked why after literally experiencing a fiery trial of their faith. They and their five children were driving home to Chicago after visiting their son at a college in Wisconsin. Without warning, part of the rear end of a truck broke off, struck their van, and ruptured its gas tank. Instantly their van became an inferno. The parents suffered severe burns but managed to exit their vehicle, but all five children perished in the flames. Later in a television interview the pastor and his wife testified to God's grace and love. They shared with viewers the comfort they drew from knowing they would see their children in heaven.

The manner in which this couple coped with the horrendous loss of their five children spoke volumes about the hope of heaven and the reality of God's eternal love. Like the apostle Paul, they cherished God's promise that his grace is sufficient (2 Cor. 12:9).

Jesus told a story about a sower and seed. Some seed fell on rocky ground and did not develop roots. He compared this seed to those who hear God's Word but fail to accept it with true faith. When trouble or persecution strikes, these mere professors of faith quickly fall away (Mark 4:16–17). Trials, then, separate real faith from phony faith.

The apostle Peter wrote his first letter to believers scattered by persecution throughout the Mediterranean world. The Romans had confiscated their homes, uprooted them, and forced them to become refugees. Their lives had become extremely harsh, but they had not lost their faith. Peter recalled that they "may have had to suffer grief in all kinds of trials" (1:6), but the trials proved the genuineness of their faith, even as fire refines gold and proves its genuineness (v. 7).

Having ministered more than fifty years, I have seen how the school of suffering graduates outstanding students of faith. A deacon paralyzed below the neck always praised the Lord for his goodness and never complained. His life of true faith touched all who knew him. A husband whose son was killed in a tragic gun accident and whose wife succumbed to liver cancer speaks of God's grace and love. A missionary wife sees her husband shot and killed by terrorists in the Philippines and writes her story affirming God's wisdom and grace. A young woman loses her mother to cancer and her father to a heart attack a few months later but testifies that she wants to serve the Lord all the days of her life. A father learns that a car accident has taken the life of one teenage son and left the other son critically injured. He expresses his

desire that the Lord will restore to him "a crescent of joy."

Trials strengthen our faith by prodding us to pray. How much praying would we do if life were all sunshine and no rain? As a wise Christian observed, when we are on our backs we are looking up.

Read some of the psalms David wrote when King Saul scoured the wilderness, hoping to find him and kill him. You will see how David exercised his faith by praying. Hear, for example, his words of prayer in Psalm 63:1: "O God, you are my God, earnestly I seek you; my soul thirsts for you, my body longs for you, in a dry and weary land where there is no water."

Another psalmist, Asaph, wrestled with the issue of God's fairness. Feeling alone and baffled by the prosperity of the wicked, he turned to God for answers. He wrote in Psalm 73:28, "But as for me, it is good to be near God. I have made the Sovereign LORD my refuge; I will tell of all your deeds."

Perform a brief honesty check! When have you prayed most earnestly and intently—when everything was sunny or when everything was stormy? Don't you agree that trouble drew you close to God and strengthened your faith?

I encountered far more trials shortly after becoming a Christian than I had encountered in my entire pre-Christian life. "Why am I having so much trouble?" I asked my Christian friends. Unanimously they responded by quoting Romans 8:28 (KJV): "All things work together for good to them that love God." *What good can possibly come from the rotten things that are happening to me?* I asked myself.

Only later did I realize my friends had not quoted Romans 8:28 in its entirety. The rest of the verse says, "to them who are the called according to his purpose." I learned that God's "purpose" was to conform me "to the image [likeness] of his Son" (v. 29 KJV). Eureka! God uses even "sufferings" (trials), mentioned in verse 18, to develop Christlike character in his people.

An observer examined exquisite hand-carved horses and watched the craftsman whittle away at another carving. "Sir," he asked, "how can you create such beautiful horses out of wood?"

"Easy," the craftsman responded. "I take a block of wood and whittle away everything that isn't horse."

Similarly, our heavenly Father, the Master Craftsman, chips away from our lives everything that isn't Christ. But he doesn't use a blade; he uses trials.

Genuine faith uses trials as motivational devices whereby we long for heaven. They teach us that a better day awaits us and point our eyes toward heaven. The apostle Paul assured us that "we do not lose heart. Though outwardly we are wasting away, yet inwardly we are being renewed day by day. For our light and momentary troubles are achieving for us an eternal glory that far outweighs them all. So we fix our eyes not on what is seen, but on what is unseen. For what is seen is temporary, but what is unseen is eternal" (2 Cor. 4:16–18).

Peter affirmed this truth when he urged his readers to look by faith beyond their troubles to the return of Christ. He wrote: "These [trials] have come so that your faith—of greater worth than gold, which perishes even though refined by fire—may be proved genuine and may result in praise, glory and honor when Jesus Christ is revealed" (1 Peter 1:7).

A hymn writer captures the optimism of Peter's words. He wrote:

> It will be worth it all when we see Jesus.
>
> It will be worth it all when we see Christ.
>
> One glimpse of His dear face
>
> All trials will erase.
>
> So bravely run the race, 'til we see Christ.

A young boy floated a toy sailboat on a pond. Suddenly, after the little boat had reached the center of the pond, the afternoon breeze stopped. All was calm, and the boy's sailboat was motionless.

Seeing the youngster's despair, an older boy began to throw stones toward the sailboat. The youngster cringed, thinking the older boy was adding insult to injury. As he watched, though, he noticed that each stone landed on the far side of the sailboat and caused a ripple to form and push the sailboat in his direction.

Eventually, the last stone had done its work, and the sailboat was within the youngster's grasp.

Trials are not evil. We may think God is throwing stones at us when trials come our way, but our loving heavenly Father is simply using the trials to draw us closer to heaven's shore.

Some may think that faith is never having to say life is tough, but faith is really never having to say God's love and grace are inadequate.

Misconception Nine

※

JUDGE NOT

P resident Bill Clinton's sexual escapades with a young intern initially shocked the nation and the world, yet over time many adults developed a laissez-faire attitude about it. They responded to the sullying of the presidency by asking nonchalantly, "Who are we to judge?"

Their response wasn't surprising, given the fact that we live in a post-Christian, postmodern era of no or very few moral absolutes. Sin is often perceived as the exercising of a value judgment on an immoral act rather than the act itself. For example, a congregation that dismisses a pastor because he had an affair may come under harsh criticism. Other congregations may describe the dismissal as a harsh, unloving, and judgmental action. The reasoning goes like this: "Who do those people think they are? They should have forgiven the pastor and allowed him to continue his ministry. After all, we are all sinners. Who are we to judge?"

JUDGE NOT

The question usually spins off an interpretation of Matthew 7:1, "Do not judge, or you too will be judged." This command issued by Jesus in the Sermon on the Mount deserves our careful attention. Does it forbid all judging? Must we shrug our shoulders meekly and blink twice at wrongdoing? Or was Jesus referring only to a specific kind of judging? To find the correct answer we must examine the context.

Matthew 7:1 lies in the context of Jesus' teachings about true righteousness, the righteousness that characterizes his kingdom and its citizens. True righteousness exceeds "that of the Pharisees and the teachers of the law" (5:20). It fulfills the spirit of the law, whereas the righteousness of the Pharisees and the teachers of the law was simply a facade. They pretended to be righteous by appearing to keep the Mosaic law and hundreds of man-made additions to the law. They performed religious acts to be seen and applauded (6:1). When they gave to the needy, trumpets sounded to announce their giving (v. 2). When they prayed, they chose to pray in prominent public places (v. 5). When they fasted, they "disfigure[d] their faces to show men they [were] fasting" (v. 16). Jesus called them "hypocrites" (vv. 2, 5, 16).

One segment of Pharisees was known as "Bruised Pharisees," because they received bruises from walking into trees. Why did they do such a stupid, clumsy thing? Because they wanted to appear righteous! When a woman approached, they ~~seized the opportunity~~ to pretend they were too holy even to glance at a woman. So they would close their eyes and intentionally walk into a tree. Hence the bruises.

The Pharisees and scribes (teachers of the law) opposed Jesus and his teachings. Their false sense of righteousness contrasted sharply with the righteousness Jesus associated with the Father's kingdom and innate righteousness (v. 33).

Jesus described hypocrites as judging, that is, distinguishing or deciding by a faulty standard of righteousness. Religious hypocrites, like the scribes and Pharisees, find no fault in themselves but see miniscule faults in others. They look down their noses at others but never examine their own imperfections. Jesus asked, "Why do you look at the speck of sawdust in your brother's eye and pay no attention to the plank in your own eye? How can you say to your brother, 'Let me take the speck out of your eye,' when all the time there is a plank in your own eye?" (7:3–4). He instructed, "You hypocrite, first take the plank out of your own eye, and then you will see clearly to remove the speck from your brother's eye" (v. 5).

Luke 18:9–14 discloses a clear example of a Pharisee's hypocritical judgment. He and a tax collector entered the temple to pray. The Pharisee took great pride in his self-righteousness. The tax collector claimed no righteousness. When he prayed, the Pharisee thanked God that he was "not like other men—robbers, evildoers, adulterers—or even like this tax collector" (v. 11). He flashed his religious credentials, reminding God that he fasted twice a week and tithed "all I get." Apparently he had gone to the temple for praise and worship: He worshipped himself and praised himself. The tax collector had gone to the temple to confess that he was a sinner and to cast himself on God's mercy. Verse 13 reveals, "He would not even look up to heaven, but beat his breast and said, 'God, have mercy on me a sinner.'"

God, who peers through hypocrisy and examines the heart, rejected the Pharisee's "worship" but responded to the tax collector's contrition. Jesus said the tax collector "went home justified before God. For everyone who exalts himself will be humbled, and he who humbles himself will be exalted" (v. 14).

A self-appointed judge of her neighbors' children, lifestyle, and care of their property (doesn't every neighborhood have a self-appointed judge?) looked out her kitchen window and was appalled to see splotches of dirt on the laundry hanging on her next-door neighbor's clothesline. Promptly, she marched next door and read the riot act to her neighbor. But when the two women entered the backyard and examined the laundry, they couldn't find even a speck of dirt. The splotches were actually on the outside of the busybody's kitchen window.

Jesus assured his Sermon on the Mount audience that "in the same way you judge others, you will be judged" (Matt. 7:2). Some Bible commentators suggest this statement indicates that God will judge us on the basis of how we judge others. But this interpretation can't be right. If we judge others falsely, will God judge us falsely? Of course not! He is just, and his judgment is always according to truth (see Ps. 75:2; Isa. 11: 3–4; Acts 17:31; 2 Tim. 4:8; Rev. 19:11). A better interpretation seems to be that others will judge us the way we judge them. If we are critical and rush to judgment without weighing the facts, others will be critical of us.

Mr. Stovelli, a street person, received a gospel tract, read it, and believed in Christ as his Savior. The following Sunday he entered an evangelical church known for its strong support of foreign missions. Somehow, he had obtained a Bible and carried it between the right side of his chest and upper right arm. His clothes were dirty and shabby, but he felt clean inside. As he walked to a seat, he noticed a mural above the platform. It read: "To love God and to share his love with the whole world." Mr. Stovelli noticed something else too—people were casting disapproving looks at him. No one had greeted him, and he wondered if anyone would say hello on his way out. No one did.

The congregation Mr. Stovelli encountered typifies the kind of hypocritical judging Jesus condemned. It advertised its love for the whole world but failed to love a new believer in shabby clothes. It had judged him to be unworthy of its love.

If we follow Jesus' counsel about judging, we will not pass judgment on anyone without first searching our own life for the very thing we condemn in the other person's life. If we find it, we must uproot it and discard it. To do less is to be hypocritical.

According to John 8:3–4, some scribes and Pharisees brought an adulteress to Jesus to see how he would decide her fate. They explained that she had been caught in the act of adultery and that the law of Moses commanded that she be stoned. "Now what do you say?" they asked Jesus (v. 5).

Jesus did not offer a verbal reply. Instead, he bent down and started to write on the ground with his finger. When the scribes and Pharisees kept questioning him, Jesus stood up and said, "If any one of you is without sin, let him be the first to throw a stone at her" (v. 7).

He bent down and wrote on the ground again, and as he wrote, the scribes and Pharisees walked away. Finally, only Jesus and the woman remained (vv. 8–9).

"Where are they?" Jesus asked the woman. "Has no one condemned you?" (v. 10).

"No one, sir," she answered (v. 11).

"Then neither do I condemn you," Jesus told her (v. 11).

What? Did Jesus take the who-am-I-to-judge way out of a messy situation? Absolutely not! He did not overlook the woman's sin but offered her forgiveness and the opportunity to live free of her sin. "Go now and leave your life of sin," he commanded her (v. 11).

It is wrong to judge in a self-righteous, hypocritical way, but it is not wrong to judge.

The Bible instructs believers to make judgments. Soon after telling his audience, "Do not judge" (Matt. 7:1), Jesus commanded, "Watch out for false prophets" (v. 15). Obviously, he expected his audience to distinguish between truth and error. But he set the criteria for judging. He explained that false prophets can be identified by their fruit (v. 16). Whereas teachers of truth produce good fruit, teachers of error produce bad fruit (v. 18).

We would not be wrong to judge a religious teacher unworthy of financial support or personal loyalty if he leads an immoral lifestyle or swindles the elderly out of their meager savings or persuades his followers to sell their homes and give the proceeds to his "ministry." A whistle-blower would have been right to judge Jim Jones a teacher of error and try to avert the mass suicide he ordered in Jonestown, Guyana, in 1978. Nine hundred thirteen of his followers might still be alive if they had judged him and his teaching.

Who would have faulted Christians for deciding that Heaven's Gate cult leader, sixty-five-year-old Marshall Herff Applewhite, was a false teacher? Apparently he taught his followers that the arrival of Hale-Bopp Comet in 1997 signaled their imminent removal to another world. Police found thirty-nine Heaven's Gate followers dead in a mansion in Rancho Santa Fe, California. They had ingested phenobarbital and alcohol, and then plastic bags had been placed over the heads of all but two of the cult members.

And should we not judge the error perpetrated by Jehovah's Witnesses? They deny the deity of Jesus and also claim that he did not rise bodily from the dead.

If we obey Jesus' command "Watch out for false prophets," we will cherish the truth and defend it. The apostle Jude informed his readers: "I felt I had to write and urge you to contend for the faith that was once for all entrusted to the saints. For certain men whose condemnation was written about long ago have secretly slipped in among you" (Jude vv. 3–4). Now, note Jude's appropriate judging: "They are godless men, who change the grace of our God into a license for immorality and deny Jesus Christ our only Sovereign and Lord" (v. 4).

Jude's judgment was not based on self-righteousness but on the immoral lifestyle and corrupt teaching of those whom he judged. That kind of judgment is appropriate today as well.

~ 119 ~

Before Israel entered Canaan, a land inhabited by pagans and dominated by false religion, she received criteria from the Lord for judging between truth and error:

> But a prophet who presumes to speak in my name any-
> thing I have not commanded him to say, or a prophet who
> speaks in the name of other gods, must be put to death.
>
> You may say to yourselves, "How can we know when
> a message has not been spoken by the LORD?" If what a
> prophet proclaims in the name of the LORD does not take
> place or come true, that is a message the LORD has not
> spoken. That prophet has spoken presumptuously. Do not
> be afraid of him. (Deut. 18:20–22)

In Galatians, Paul chided his readers for deviating from the grace of Christ. Certain religious teachers had infiltrated the Galatian churches and brought along a message of salvation based on works. Instead of judging those teachers as false, the Galatians had accepted them. Paul insisted that there is only one gospel, the gospel of grace that he had preached to them. He implored the Galatians to distinguish between truth and error and reject both the error and the teachers of error. He wrote in 1:8–9: "But even if we or an angel from heaven should preach a gospel other than the one we preached to you, let him be eternally condemned! As we have already said, so now I say again: If anybody is preaching to you a gospel other than what you accepted, let him be eternally condemned!"

Two cultured and attractive young women became temporary residents of a town where I was a pastor. They rented a studio, opened a charm school, and offered high school girls free instruction. However, the charm school was simply a means to an end. The two young women were cult missionaries. Once the high schoolers were a captive audience, they introduced their religious teachings.

A family arranged a meeting in its home between the charming missionaries and me, so we could discuss our beliefs. The meeting became a series of meetings in which I used Scripture to answer the missionaries' avowed beliefs. Although the discussions ended without my persuading the young women to accept biblical beliefs, the family members indicated they had learned the value of using the Bible to judge religious teachings.

The Bible is, after all, the standard of distinguishing truth and error. Jesus declared, "Your word is truth" (John 17:17). Since the Bible is truth, any teaching that contradicts it or adds to it is error. Therefore, we can make valid judgments about unbiblical religious teachings. Isaiah 8:20 states, "To the law and to the testimony! If they speak not according to this word, they have no light of dawn."

In his old age, the apostle John, who heard Jesus' Sermon on the Mount, summoned believers to make judgments about truth and error. In 1 John 4:1 he challenged: "Dear friends, do not believe every spirit, but test the spirits to see whether they are from God, because many false prophets have gone out into the world." On a similar note, Paul charged the Thessalonian believers to "test everything" (1 Thess. 5:21). Writing to the Corinthians, he warned against false prophets and described Satan as one who "masquerades as an angel of light" (2 Cor. 11:14). Obviously, someone who appears at a Christian's doorstep as a well-mannered, well-groomed religious person may actually be a messenger of Satan. Only sound judgment based on Scripture will safeguard the resident's faith.

In another Scripture, Paul warned against false teachers. "Watch out for those dogs, those men who do evil, those mutilators of the flesh," he advised the Christians at Philippi (Phil. 3:2), obviously referring to the Judaizers.

But not only does the Bible teach us to make judgments about false teachers and errant doctrines, it also holds us responsible to judge immorality. In 1 Corinthians 5, Paul grieved that the church at Corinth had allowed one of its members to carry on an affair with his stepmother without being confronted (vv. 1–2). He ordered the church to discipline the offender (vv. 3–5), and reminded its members that he had written in a previous letter that they should not "associate with sexually immoral people" (v. 9), and was writing now to tell them to "not associate with anyone who calls himself a brother but is sexually immoral or greedy, an idolater or a slanderer, a drunkard or a swindler. With such a man do not even eat" (v. 11). "Are you not to judge those inside [the church]?" he asked (v. 12).

What could be clearer? God holds congregations accountable to judge immorality. Just as a police department must conduct an occasional internal investigation to discipline and even weed out bad cops, so a congregation must exercise discipline for the sake of purity and public testimony. If it fails to judge immorality, a congregation loses God's blessing and credibility in the community. And contrary to the belief that a church that judges immorality will surely scare people off, it may actually lose an opportunity to grow dramatically.

The early church at Jerusalem judged sin in its midst. Case in point: the disciplining of Ananias and Sapphira, who had conspired to lie to the Holy Spirit. On behalf of the church Peter confronted this couple individually and confronted their sin. The result? Ananias fell down dead, and then Sapphira fell down dead (Acts 5:1–10). Great fear—the fear of God—seized the whole church, but "more and more men and women believed in the Lord and were added to their number" (v. 14).

Just as fire purifies gold, so the fire of self-judgment purifies a congregation. The judgment must be exercised in love and with a desire to restore offenders, but it must be as thorough as fire. It must not pass over some sinning church members because they give well or are related to a church officer. It must burn the dross wherever it finds it. If a congregation refuses to take disciplinary action while asking, "Who are we to judge?" its love for Christ and his Word will become as a cold as ice. Who would want to worship in a freezer?

Late one night, a small church was engulfed in flames, and a crowd had gathered to witness the tragedy. Among those who had gathered were a deacon and an agnostic.

"Wally," the deacon called to the agnostic, "I never expected to see you at church!"

"Well," said Wally, "this is the first time I've seen the church on fire."

How many of our fellow citizens might start attending church if they see a holy fire blazing in our hearts? How many will stay away if we fail to judge error and sin?

Misconception Ten

✳

JESUS MIGHT JUST SAY, "I NEVER KNEW YOU!"

A couple of years ago, a distant female relative in Canada contacted me for information about my brothers, my children, my grandchildren, my deceased parents, and me. I had never met her but appreciated her interest in compiling a family history of the Dyets. My parents had emigrated from Scotland to Canada twice. My father moved to Hamilton, Ontario, Canada, around 1927, and then summoned my mother to follow him to Canada and get married. (I can't pinpoint the years because my parents didn't tell me much, if anything, about that period of their lives.) Mom took Dad up on the proposal. They married in Hamilton, Ontario, and in 1930, my brother Bill was born there. A couple of years later, Mom and Dad returned to Scotland, where I was born in 1935. Apparently, the call of Canada came rushing over the Atlantic again, because my parents returned to Canada in 1939, this time with my older brother and me in tow. They settled in Ottawa, where my brother Bruce was born in 1940.

Because I was so young when I left Scotland, I did not get to know my relatives there. However, Dad had relatives in Ottawa, whom I had a chance to know for a short while, but one year later my parents moved almost four hundred miles from Ottawa to St. Catharines. So I grew up knowing little about any Dyets other than my parents and two brothers.

I always regretted this fact, so I was happy to learn that a distant relative had taken on the project of identifying members of the Dyet family tree. However, the project involved only those who had settled and raised families in Canada and the United States. I still have no knowledge of relatives living among the highland heather or in lowland towns. Not knowing them saddens me, but I can live without knowing them.

What is not only sad but also tragic is the fact that so many people around the world do not know Jesus Christ. They may know something about him from singing Christmas carols or hearing a Christian broadcast or from some other experience, but they do not know him. If they die without knowing him, they will have lost the opportunity to enjoy a beautiful life on earth and an even better one in heaven.

Will Jesus say to every unbeliever, "I never knew you"? Might he say that to you? For the answer, we need to examine the context in which he spoke those fateful words. It is Matthew 7:15–23, near the end of Jesus'

Sermon on the Mount. In his sermon, Jesus exposed the hypocrisy of Israel's religious leaders. They put on an elaborate show of religious fervor and ceremonial observance, but their hearts were not right with God. Instead of repenting and trusting in him for righteousness, they felt no need to repent or rely on anything but their self-proclaimed religious credentials. Jesus had warned his audience not to "do your 'acts of righteousness' before men, to be seen of by them" (Matt. 6:1).

He cited hypocritical giving, praying, and fasting as the kinds of worthless displays of religion that mark false religious leaders. Hypocrites in Jesus' day enjoyed having trumpets announce their giving to the needy. They basked in the public attention (v. 2). They also chose to pray on busy street corners, because they wanted to be seen by as many people as possible (v. 5). When they fasted, they disfigured their faces.

God cannot tolerate hypocrisy. In his prayer of confession, King David rightly observed, "Surely you desire truth in the inner parts" (Ps. 51:6). Jesus identified false prophets as ferocious wolves wearing sheep's clothing (Matt. 7:15). He also compared them to bad trees bearing bad fruit and deserving to be "cut down and thrown into the fire" (v. 19).

In the end-time, there will come the defining moment of God's judgment, and Jesus will encounter many "applicants" for kingdom citizenship. They will cite reasons they believe qualify them for citizenship. They will not point to what Jesus did for them by dying on the cross but to what they felt they had done for Jesus. They will say, "Lord, Lord, did we not prophesy in your name, and in your name drive out demons and perform many miracles?" (v. 22).

Years ago I worked in a small building while a bigger building was under construction. The Human Resources Department occupied three cubicles near mine. One was directly across from my cubicle; the other two were on my left and right. During a vigorous employee-hiring campaign, the HR cubicles were bustling with interviews. A parade of job applicants filed in and out, and I could not help hearing them describe the skills they proposed to contribute for the good of the company. Many left no self-compliment at the entrance. They were strong leaders, creative, team players, resourceful, cooperative, diligent, productive, loyal, can-do men and women whose work would far exceed expectations. They had instituted cost-saving programs at their previous workplace. They had accomplished incredible tasks and left the competition in the dust. Each applicant firmly believed the company would benefit enormously if it hired him or her. Upon hearing all the braggadocio, I wondered why the applicants did not run for the presidency of the United States.

When Jesus "interviews" applicants for his kingdom, he will encounter many applicants like those I overheard.

They will boast about their personal greatness and outstanding "tract" record, but the boasting will not fool Jesus. He will turn them down with a resolute "I never knew you. Away from me, you evildoers!" (Matt. 7:23).

A couple of plausible explanations may help us understand the claims about prophesying, casting out demons, and performing many miracles—all in Jesus' name (v. 22).

First, these supernatural wonders may be attributed to satanic power. The Bible's prophesies assure us the end-times will introduce numerous false prophets and deceivers who will try to pass themselves off as Israel's Messiah. Jesus predicted: "At that time if anyone says to you, 'Look, here is the Christ!' or, 'There he is!' do not believe it. For false Christs and false prophets will appear and perform great signs and miracles to deceive even the elect—if that were possible" (Matt. 24:23–24). We know the false prophet described in Revelation 13 will cast himself in a messianic role by performing amazing feats by satanic power. Revelation 13:13 reports, "And he performed great and miraculous signs, even causing fire to come down from heaven to earth in full view of men." Verse 15 says, "He was given power to give breath to the image of the first beast, so that it could speak." All the world loves a show, and Satan will empower end-time deceivers to put on a really big show to attract followers, just as he did with Pharaoh's wicked magicians (Ex. 7:10–13).

Second, the claims about prophesying, casting out demons, and performing miracles may be simply empty claims. The history of religion includes charlatans who duped their followers by making grandiose, but unfounded, claims of religious power. Of course, religious fakes cannot fool Jesus. He knows the human heart and judges as "the faithful and true witness" (Rev. 3:14).

Matthew 25:1–12 offers further insight into the timing of Jesus' words, "I never knew you." He commented in this passage that "at that time [the time of his return to earth; see Matt. 24:44] the kingdom of heaven will be like ten virgins who took their lamps and went out to meet the bridegroom" (25:1). According to Jesus' parable of the ten virgins, five were foolish and five were wise. When the ten virgins went to meet the bridegroom, the five foolish ones did not take any extra oil for their lamps, whereas the five wise ones did (vv. 3–4).

All ten grew tired as they waited for the bridegroom to arrive for the wedding banquet. Overcome by drowsiness, they fell asleep (v. 5). At midnight, shouts jolted them from sleep. People were yelling, "Here's the bridegroom! Come out to meet him!" (v. 6).

The ten virgins trimmed their lamps, but only the five wise ones had enough oil to fire up their lamps. The others had to go searching for oil they could purchase. And while they searched, the bridegroom arrived and, accompanied

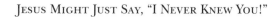

by the five wise virgins, entered the banquet hall. Once they had entered, the entry door closed (vv. 7–10).

Later, the five foolish virgins returned and called, "Sir! Sir! ... Open the door for us!" (v. 11).

"I tell you the truth," the bridegroom responded, "I don't know you" (v. 12).

Those who heard Jesus' parable would have understood the wedding customs of the day. Traditionally, a wedding took place in the bride's house, after which the bridegroom and bride would lead a procession to the bridegroom's house, where a marriage supper would take place. Jesus, the Bridegroom, will come in the air someday for his bride, the church.[2] Like the five wise virgins, she will be seated at the wedding banquet, the marriage supper of the Lamb, but the unbelieving pretenders, like the five foolish virgins, are shut out.

The biblical writers Matthew, Luke, and John allude to this celebration:

> I [Jesus] say to you that many will come from the east and the west, and will take their places at the feast with Abraham, Isaac and Jacob in the kingdom of heaven. (Matt. 8:11)
>
> He will reply, "I don't know you or where you come from. Away from me, all of you evildoers!" There will be weeping there, and gnashing of teeth, when you see Abraham, Isaac and Jacob and all the prophets in the kingdom of God, but you yourselves thrown out.

> People will come from east and west and north and
> south, and will take their places at the feast in the king-
> dom of God. (Luke 13:27–29)
>
> Then I heard what sounded like a great multitude, like the
> roar of rushing waters and like loud peals of thunder,
> shouting: "Hallelujah! For our Lord God Almighty reigns.
> Let us rejoice and be glad and give him glory! For the wed-
> ding of the Lamb has come, and his bride has made herself
> ready. Fine linen, bright and clean, was given her to wear."
> (Fine linen stands for the righteous acts of the saints.) Then
> the angel said to me, "Write: 'Blessed are those who are
> invited to the wedding supper of the Lamb!'" And he
> added, "These are the true words of God." (Rev. 19:6–9)

Clearly, at his return to establish his earthly kingdom, Jesus will make a decisive distinction between those who truly know him and those who merely profess to know him. Those who know him are "sheep" that entered the fold through Jesus, the one and only gate (John 10:7, 9). Jesus declared, "I am the good shepherd; I know my sheep and my sheep know me" (v. 14).

We can conclude from passages related to Matthew 7:21–23 that Jesus will not allow into his kingdom those who merely pretend to be his followers. He "will tell them plainly, 'I never knew you. Away from me, you evildoers!'" (v. 23).

Based on what Jesus taught following this statement of rejection, we must raise a warning flag for all who

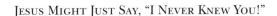
know Jesus' teachings but not Jesus. He related a story of two builders and compared them to two different kinds of hearers of his words. One builder was wise. He built his house on "the rock" (v. 24). When rains pummeled his house and floods swept over it and wind struck it violently, it stood secure on its firm foundation. Jesus said everyone who hears his words and "puts them into practice" is like this wise builder (v. 24). Another builder built his house on sand (v. 26). Pelting rain, rising floods, and relentless wind demolished this builder's house (v. 27). Jesus compared everyone who hears his words but fails to put them into practice to this foolish builder (v. 26).

Jesus must have been addressing the scribes and Pharisees directly, but indirectly all who hear his words and ignore them. The warning applies today to all who hear Jesus' words but ignore or reject them. Someday, everything they have built, whether it be a materialistic life, a life of pleasure, a life of popularity or fame, or one of academic pursuit, will come crashing down. Even a life of empty profession of faith—a hypocritical life— will crash under the weight of Jesus' incontrovertible judgment.

According to a humorous, but applicable, anecdote, several teenage pranksters decided to play a practical joke on a country church known for its emotionally charged worship. They outfitted one of their buddies in a devil's costume: red suit, black tail, pointed ears, horns, and a

~ 133 ~

pitchfork. Silently, they crept up to the church and eaves-dropped on the worship.

The worship grew louder and louder as the congregation shook, clapped, and shouted. When the worship reached a fever pitch, the pranksters opened the church's front door and shoved the devil into the building.

Down the center aisle slinked the devil, extending his pitchfork menacingly. Swoosh went the churchgoers as they rushed out the exit doors and bolted through the windows. Everybody catapulted from the church. Well, everybody but one very portly deacon in his midsixties. Just as he was about to enter the aisle, his belly got wedged between two pews.

Seeing the devil with pitchfork pointed at him, the deacon screamed, "Just a minute, Mr. Devil. Stop right where you are. I want you to know I have been a member of this church for forty-two years, but I've been on your side the whole time."

Not humorous at all is the fact that many churchgoers today resemble the deacon. For years they have attended church regularly, listened to Jesus' words, participated in the weekly offering, taken Communion, and perhaps taught Sunday school or served on the church board or sung in the choir; but they have been on the Devil's side the whole time. They have never trusted in Jesus as their Savior. If they die without knowing Jesus, they will hear Jesus say to them in effect, "Depart from me. I never knew you."

In the final analysis, religious works and good deeds cannot save even one person. The apostle Paul informed the Ephesians that God saves by grace through faith and added that salvation is "the gift of God—not by works, so that no one can boast" (Eph. 2:8–9).

Named after Israel's first king, Saul, Paul (formerly Saul of Tarsus) knew firsthand the truth he expressed in writing. Before being saved by grace through faith in Jesus Christ, Paul had buried himself in religion and taken great personal pride in his religious credentials (Phil. 3:4–6). In accordance with Mosaic law, he had been circumcised when he was eight days old. He was an Israelite (a member of God's chosen race). He belonged to the tribe of Benjamin, famous for its fighting ability and loyalty to King David. Unlike Jews who observed Gentile customs and spoke a Gentile language, Paul was a Hebrew of the Hebrews (v. 5). He had been a Pharisee, fully devoted to the law. No one's zeal for the Jewish religion had exceeded his. He had demonstrated white-hot zeal by persecuting the church. Further, he had faultlessly adhered to legalistic religion.

But Paul had learned on the Damascus road that all his religious credentials and deeds failed to make him righteous in God's sight. He discarded all his religious baggage, believed in Christ for salvation, and testified, "I consider everything a loss compared to the surpassing greatness of knowing Christ Jesus my Lord" (v. 8).

Personal knowledge of Christ as Savior assured Paul that Jesus would never say to him, "Depart from me." To the contrary, Paul testified in 2 Timothy 1:12: "I know whom I have believed, and am convinced that he is able to guard what I have entrusted to him for that day."

I have had the privilege of preaching not only in churches but also in rescue missions and prisons. Often, the response to the gospel has been better among convicts and derelicts than among churchgoers. The reason is simple. Convicts and derelicts readily admit their shortcomings and need of salvation, whereas few unbelieving churchgoers admit their guilt and need. Churchgoing hypocrites try to hide their true condition behind a facade of religiosity. But they cannot hide from God.

Near the end of Revelation, the last book of the Bible, the final drama of history unfolds. God pulls the curtain back to give us a glimpse of the drama. The apostle John narrates the scene. He identifies "a great white throne and him who was seated on it. Earth and sky fled from his presence, and there was no place for them" (20:11).

This is the final judgment of all unbelievers, including hypocrites who merely pretended to know Jesus. These arraigned lost souls try to flee from the judgment. They learn, however, as Jonah did a long time ago, that you can run from God but you cannot hide. They find no hiding place and must appear before the righteous Judge, who judges them according to their works (v. 12).

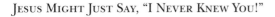

The open record of their works shows they are unfit for heaven. Then, all who stand before the throne of judgment are sentenced to the lake of fire because their names do not appear in the Book of Life (v. 15).

Could the Lord say to you someday, "Depart from me. I never knew you"? You alone can answer this question. If you know him as your Savior, you will hear him welcome you to heaven. If you pass from this life without knowing him as your Savior, he will banish you from his presence forever.

The apostle John explained the entire issue of eternal life in a simple formula: "He who has the Son has life; he who does not have the Son of God does not have life" (1 John 5:12).

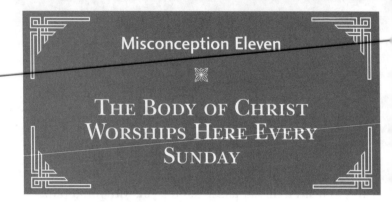

P astor Mike greeted the congregation warmly. "We
are so glad you chose to worship at Good News
Church. We welcome you and pray that the worship will
lift you spiritually and emotionally and be the highlight of
your week. If you are visiting for the first time, please plan
on making today the beginning of a long and happy relationship with Good News Church. The body of Christ
worships here every Sunday morning at ten o'clock, and
we hope to see you often."

We cannot fault Pastor Mike's sincerity and friendli-
ness, but was he correct to say, "The body of Christ
worships here every Sunday"? Just what is "the body of
Christ"?

The term is used two ways in the New Testament. The
first and more obvious meaning is the physical body of
our Lord. The apostle Paul wrote in Romans 7:4, "So, my
brothers, you also died to the law through the body of
Christ, that you might belong to another, to him who was

~ 138 ~

raised from the dead, in order that we might bear fruit to God." Paul looked back to the crucifixion and understood what Jesus accomplished for believers by sacrificing his body to free us from the penalty of sin imposed by the law. The apostle Peter affirmed this truth in 1 Peter 2:24: "He [Jesus] himself bore our sins in his body on the tree, so that we might die to sins and live for righteousness; by his wounds you have been healed."

The second use of the term, the body of Christ, applies to the church, the organism composed of all Christians. Christ is the head of the church; he dwells in the church and fills it. The Ephesian letter presents significant truths about the church, the body of Christ. According to Ephesians 1:22–23, God appointed Christ as the church's head, the church is Christ's body, and he fills it. Ephesians 2:11–22 declares that saved Jews and saved Gentiles share a union with Christ and a spiritual unity in the church. Ephesians 3:21 identifies the purpose of the church, the body of Christ. It is to bring glory to Christ. Ephesians 4:4 proclaims that the church is one body, and subsequent verses teach that Christ has gifted individuals to edify (build) the body, the church, so that she may achieve "unity in the faith and in the knowledge of the Son of God and become mature, attaining to the whole measure of the fullness of Christ" (v. 13). Ephesians 5:25–27 focuses on the church as the object of Christ's love. He died for the church "to make her holy" and to "present her to himself as a radiant church, without stain or wrinkle or any other blemish, but holy and blameless."

In 1 Corinthians 12:12–13, Paul explained how believers, regardless of their diversity, become members of the body of Christ. He wrote: "The body is a unit, though it is made up of many parts; and though all its parts are many, they form one body. So it is with Christ. For we were all baptized by one Spirit into one body—whether Jews or Greeks, slave or free—and we were all given the one Spirit to drink."

Galatians 3:27–28 affirms this truth. These verses teach: "For all of you who were baptized into Christ have clothed yourselves with Christ. There is neither Jew nor Greek, slave nor free, male nor female, for you are all one in Christ Jesus."

When a person believes in Jesus as Savior, the Holy Spirit baptizes him or her into Christ. At that moment, that person becomes a member of the church, the body of Christ. It is appropriate, however, to join a local church and to fellowship with other believers.

When the Holy Spirit descended at Pentecost and united the believers into the spiritual organism called the body of Christ, those who believed joined together as a local body of believers at Jerusalem. They functioned as a local church, devoting themselves "to the apostles' teaching and to the fellowship, to the breaking of bread and to prayer" (Acts 2:42).

No doubt, the vast majority of Christians who refer to the local church as the body of Christ do so as a slip of the tongue. They do not actually believe that their church is *the* body of Christ. However, others do honestly believe this. This belief is a tenet of their theology. They reject the belief that the body of Christ is a spiritual organism usually called "the universal church" or "the invisible church." They interpret 1 Corinthians 12:13—"baptized by one Spirit into one body"—like this:

"baptized": immersed in water

"by one Spirit": in one spirit (lowercase), suggesting agreement, unity

"into one body": membership in the local church

Those who reject the concept of the universal church generally charge that the doctrine is a Scofieldian error. Here's a sample of what Dr. C. I. Scofield wrote concerning the nature of the church:

> The Church, composed of the whole number of regenerate persons from Pentecost to the first resurrection (1 Cor. 15:52), united together and to Christ by the baptism of the Holy Spirit (1 Cor. 12:12, 13). Is the body of Christ of which He is the Head (Eph. 1:22, 23). As such, it is a holy temple for the habitation of God through the Spirit (Eph. 2:21, 22); is 'one flesh' with Christ (Eph. 5:30, 31); and espoused to Him as a chaste virgin to one husband (2 Cor. 11:2–4); and will be translated to heaven at the return of the Lord to the air (1 Thess. 4:13–17).[3]

In all fairness to those who believe the local church is the body of Christ, we ought to examine a Scripture verse that seems to support their view. Addressing the members of the Corinthian church, Paul stated: "Now you are the body of Christ, and each one of you is a part of it" (1 Cor. 12:27). Doesn't this verse seem to suggest that the church at Corinth was the body of Christ?

It does until we read it in the Greek New Testament and find that the word "the" does not appear in the verse. The Greek indicates: "Now you are Christ's body and members each in his part." Although this translation is similar to what many English Bibles state, we must understand that things may be similar without being the same. The absence of the definite article "the" does not point to the church at Corinth as *a* body of Christ, because there is only one body of Christ, not many. The quality of the noun, "body," is stressed by the absence of the definite article. The Corinthian believers shared in the character or essence of Christ's body, the church.

A similar Greek construction occurs in John 1:1. The definite article *the* does not precede "God" in the statement "and the Word was God." Jehovah's Witnesses wrongly conclude that the translation should be "and the Word was a god." But, as we have seen, the absence of the definite article emphasizes the quality of the noun. Therefore the "Word," meaning Jesus, was God in his essential nature.

Returning to the status of the Corinthian believers, we recognize they were not *the* members of Christ's body but members each in his part. They could claim membership, but they could not claim exclusive membership. Other believers in many parts of the Roman world were also members of Christ's body, the church. Indeed, all believers, whether dead or alive, from Pentecost until Christ's return, are members of the church.

To believe that every local church is the body of Christ is to believe in a plurality of bodies of Christ. To believe that only our own local church is the body of Christ is to deny the equal spiritual standing that all believers have in Christ. We are like the congregation that called themselves the Jesus only people and hung a sign outside their church building that read JESUS ONLY. One day, a severe windstorm rattled the church building and blew away the sign's first three letters, leaving US ONLY.

But further issues confront the belief that the local church is the body of Christ.

JESUS SAID HE WOULD BUILD HIS CHURCH

"And I tell you that you are Peter, and on this rock I will build my church" (Matt. 16:18). If there is no universal church body, which local church did Jesus promise to build?

Jesus Said, "The gates of Hades will not overcome [his church]" (Matt. 16:18)

Sadly, more than one local church has fallen to the attacks of Satan. Churches that used to boldly and clearly proclaim the gospel are vacant, padlocked, and in disrepair. If the local church were exclusively Christ's church, how would we explain Jesus' promise of victory over the gates of hades?

His promise must apply to the universal church, the organism called his body. Satan has been attacking this church from its inception until the present. He has hurled malicious charges against the church, unleashed vicious enemies against her, pitted destructive philosophies against her, employed godless political systems to censure or silence her, and tripped up her leaders; but the church keeps marching onward.

Confidence in the indestructibility of Jesus' church led John Newton to write the following stanza of "Glorious Things of Thee Are Spoken":

> Glorious things of thee are spoken, Zion, city of our God;
>> He whose word cannot be broken, Formed thee for His own abode.
>> On the Rock of Ages founded, What can shake thy sure repose?
>> With salvation's walls surrounded, Thou mayest smile at all thy foes.

EPHESIANS 4:4 AFFIRMS THERE IS "ONE BODY"

There is one Spirit, one hope, one Lord, one faith, one baptism, and one God and Father. If the local church were the body of Christ, which local church would that be? If every local church were the body of Christ, there would be thousands of bodies of Christ. The only reasonable conclusion is to recognize the body of Christ as an organism composed of all believers from Pentecost to the return of Christ.

First Corinthians 12:12 also refers to Christ's body, the church, calling it "a unit." The unit "is made up of many parts; and though all its parts are many, they form one body." Succeeding verses emphasize the giftedness of all who belong to the body. Like the smooth-working parts of the human body, the gifted parts of Christ's body, the church, contribute to the church's spiritual health and effectiveness.

JESUS NOT ONLY FOUNDED HIS CHURCH BUT ALSO DIRECTS AND FILLS HIS CHURCH

Ephesians 1:22–23 declares that Jesus Christ is "head over everything for the church, which is his body, the fullness of him who fills everything in every way." To limit Jesus' domain to the local church is to diminish his headship. His lordship and fullness must surely extend beyond the local church.

JESUS GAVE HIMSELF AT CALVARY FOR THE CHURCH

Ephesians 5:25 states, "Christ loved the church and gave himself up for her." Further, verses 29 and 30 allude to the church as Christ's body: "After all, no one ever hated his own body, but he feeds and cares for it, just as Christ does the church—for we are members of his body." If the local church were the body of Christ, which local church did he love and die for? Which local church does he feed and care for? Where would such restricted love, redemption, feeding, and caring leave the rest of us?

Although I disagree with those who identify the local church or the sum of local churches as the body of Christ, I applaud their esteem for the local church. Every Christian ought to identify with a local church and employ his or her gifts to edify other believers and to assist in making disciples. Clearly, Jesus authorized his followers to proclaim the gospel worldwide, to disciple all nations, to organize local churches, and to teach believers to obey him. Matthew 28:18–20 is a key passage in this regard.

> Then Jesus came to them [the disciples] and said, "All authority in heaven and on earth has been given to me. Therefore go and make disciples of all nations, baptizing them in the name of the Father and of the Son and of the Holy Spirit, and teaching them to obey everything I have commanded you. And surely I am with you always, to the very end of the age."

Every church, indeed every Christian, ought to take this challenge to heart. The Greek word for "church" is *ekklesia*, meaning *called-out ones*, but our Lord did not call us out of the world to sit on the sidelines and watch everyone else stumble blindly until they fall into eternal perdition. He called us out of the world's evil pattern of thinking and behaving, but he commissioned us to take the message of life into the world. In his High Priestly prayer Jesus talked with his Father in heaven about the role of his called-out ones. He said: "My prayer is not that you take them out of the world but that you protect them from the evil one. They are not of the world, even as I am not of it. . . . As you sent me into the world, I have sent them into the world" (John 17:15–18). Jesus does not want us to be *isolated* from the world, but he does want us to *insulated* from its evil.

Members of Christ's body, the church, serve as ambassadors for Christ. God has placed us in strategic places around the world so that we might help to establish peaceful relations between him and those who are estranged from him. As the apostle Paul shared with the Corinthians, God "gave us the ministry of reconciliation" (2 Cor. 5:18).

How well we represent our Lord as his ambassadors depends on a number of factors. (1) Does our lifestyle reflect his righteousness? (2) Do we display the fruit of the Spirit ("love, joy, peace, patience, kindness, goodness, faithfulness, gentleness and self-control" [Gal. 5:22–23])? (3) Does the way we live give unbelievers a solid reason to want to become like us by believing in Christ? (4) Do we present a solid front to unbelievers, or do they see us as a divided, bickering segment of society? How do church splits and denominational rivalries affect our message of Christ's love and our claims that Christians are one in the bonds of love?

A story about three neighboring churches in a small town may help us rethink the oneness we profess. On a hot July Sunday, all three churches had opened their windows so worshippers could catch an occasional cool breeze. Unchurched people seated on park benches nearby could hear the hymn singing. The first congregation sang "Will There Be Any Stars in My Crown?" The second congregation sang "No, Not One." The third lifted their voices and sang lustily "Oh, That Will Be Glory for Me."

Churches should not discard their doctrinal distinctiveness for the sake of feigned unity, but true believers should show the world that they love one another. Jesus said, "By this all men will know that you are my disciples, if you love one another" (John 13:35). A Pentecostal employee and a Baptist employee working for the same company will have different opinions about certain doctrines, but they can demonstrate to their unbelieving associates that they share a love for Christ and for each other. Congregations of various denominations can reach out lovingly to a community by contributing their time and resources to evangelistic efforts. Men and women who love the Lord can launch a neighborhood Bible study and agree to disagree agreeably about peripheral doctrines while majoring on sharing the good news.

In 1925, the possibility of an epidemic of diphtheria confronted the people of Nome, Alaska. In January of that year, Dr. Curtis Welch discovered seven cases of diphtheria in the area, but the town had no diphtheria antitoxin. The good doctor immediately organized a volunteer effort to fetch 300,000 units of antitoxin from Nenana to Nome by dogsled relay teams. The *Nome Nugget* of January 31, 1925, reported twenty-two cases and five deaths. The situation was looking very grim. However, on February 2, 1925, Gunnar Kaasen arrived with the antitoxin, and his lead dog, Balto, became famous.

The relay dog mushers, who were trappers and prospectors, had traversed 658 miles in snow, strong winds, and subzero temperatures to rush the life-saving serum to Nome. The quarantine that had been imposed on Nome on January 21 was lifted on February 21.

The church today would do well to rush the life-saving message of divine grace to the many thousands who face eternal death. In these perilous times we should be far more concerned about rescuing the perishing than resting in the pews.

~ *149* ~

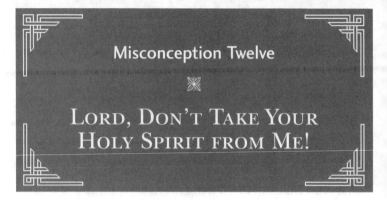

I was the guest speaker at a church known for its commitment to sound doctrine, and I was happy to learn that its children's choir was scheduled to sing before I preached.

Upon hearing the children sing, I understood why the church was proud of the kids. They sang enthusiastically, and their voices blended smoothly. Their words were distinct, and their smiles captivated the congregation. But what they sang contradicted the church's doctrinal position and sent the wrong message not only to the congregation but also to the children themselves. The words "Cast me not away from thy presence; and take not thy Holy Spirit from me" were completely out of tune with New Testament teaching.

But aren't those words scriptural? What could possibly be wrong with singing scriptural words?

King David framed those words in his well-known prayer of confession. Psalm 51 includes the whole prayer,

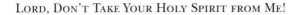

and verse 11 gives the words the children's choir sang so well but so inappropriately.

David had committed adultery with Bathsheba, and the guilt blighted his soul, stabbed his conscience, troubled his mind, and drained his energy. He feared that God might abandon him if he failed to repent and confess his sin. Perhaps he recalled that the Spirit of the Lord had departed from his predecessor, King Saul. First Samuel 16:14 states: "Now the Spirit of the Lord had departed from Saul, and an evil spirit from the Lord tormented him."

Unlike Saul, David presented a broken and contrite heart to the Lord, confronted the ugliness of his sin, acknowledged his guilt, and cried out for renewed fellowship with the Lord. He believed that God would not despise a broken and contrite heart (Ps. 51:17), and he was right. We know from Psalm 32 that God did not abandon David, nor did he withdraw his Spirit from him. Joyfully, David reported: "I acknowledged my sin to you and did not cover up my iniquity. I said, 'I will confess my transgressions to the Lord'—and you forgave the guilt of my sin" (v. 5).

Occasionally, in Old Testament times, the Holy Spirit came upon individuals and later left them, although he did dwell in a few. At Pentecost, he came upon all who believed in Jesus and since then has dwelled in every believer. In the Old Testament the Holy Spirit filled select individuals and equipped them for specific tasks. Since Pentecost, the Holy Spirit has been giving spiritual gifts to individual believers instead of to only a select group of believers.

In Exodus 31:2–5 the Lord informed Moses, "See, I have chosen Bezalel son of Uri, the son of Hur, of the tribe of Judah, and I have filled him with the Spirit of God, with skill, ability and knowledge in all kinds of crafts—to make artistic designs for work in gold, silver and bronze, to cut and set stones, to work in wood, and to engage in all kinds of craftsmanship." Thus filled and equipped by the Spirit, Bezalel would superintend the constructing and furnishing of the tabernacle.

Since Pentecost, the Lord has been building a tabernacle or temple of believers. We call it the church. The apostle Paul asked the Corinthian believers, "Don't you know that you yourselves are God's temple and that God's Spirit lives in you?" (1 Cor. 3:16). In 1 Peter 2:5 the apostle Peter wrote: "You also, like living stones, are being built into a spiritual house." However, all believers serve a "Bezalel" role, because the Spirit has gifted all of us for the task of building God's spiritual house (see Rom. 12:3–8 and Eph. 4:7–13).

Here are a few Old Testament reports of the Spirit's coming upon individuals: Judges 6:34 reports that "the Spirit of the LORD came upon Gideon." Judges 14:6 says, "The Spirit … came upon [Samson] in power." First

Samuel 10:10 announces, "The Spirit of God came upon him [Saul] in power." First Samuel 16:13 reports that "the Spirit of the LORD came upon David in power." First Chronicles 12:18 declares: "Then the Spirit came upon Amasai, chief of the Thirty." And 2 Chronicles 24:20 says: "Then the Spirit of God came upon Zechariah son of Jehoiada the priest."

With the formation of the church on the day of Pentecost, there came an end to the phenomenon of the Holy Spirit's coming upon select individuals. However, the book of Acts records several events in which the Spirit came upon groups.

First, he came upon all the believers who had gathered together in Jerusalem in anticipation of the Spirit's arrival (1:4–5). According to Acts 2 the Spirit descended on these believers, filled them, and endowed them with the ability to declare God's wonders in languages they had never learned. Peter, the spokesman for the believers, explained to the Jews gathered for the Feast of Pentecost that God had poured out his Spirit in fulfillment of prophecy.

Later, a group of Samaritan believers received the Holy Spirit when the apostles Peter and John—both Jews—prayed for them and placed their hands on them (Acts 8:14–17). This event signified that God had accepted the Samaritan believers into the church just as he had accepted Jewish believers.

Acts 10:44–47 records another occasion when a group of believers received the Spirit. It happened in the home of Cornelius, a Gentile. The Spirit came upon all who heard Peter's message about forgiveness through faith in Jesus. All the recipients of the Spirit were Gentiles, and the event convinced Peter that God had accepted Gentiles into the church.

We read in Acts 19:1–7 about another instance of the Spirit's coming upon a group. In this case, the recipients of the Spirit were Jewish disciples of John the Baptist. As soon as they learned from Paul that Jesus was the Messiah John had predicted, they believed in Jesus and were baptized. When Paul then placed his hands on them, they received the Spirit, spoke in tongues, and prophesied. These two phenomena validated Paul's message and linked this Jewish group to the church founded at Pentecost.

Now that God had given evidence that Samaritan and Gentile believers were united together in one body, the church, there would be no further descending of the Spirit on believers.

Jesus had foretold a brand-new relationship between the Spirit and every believer. The Spirit, he said in John 14:15–17, would not only be *with* believers *forever* but also *in* them.

The promised Spirit would be "another Counselor," Jesus assured his own. "Another" and "Counselor" are significant words. Two words in the Greek New Testament are translated "another." *Allos* (another) means another of the same kind. *Heteros* (another) means another of a different kind. Perhaps we can distinguish the meanings by thinking about a backyard cookout. Joe prefers rib eye steak, whereas Jerry prefers T-bone, but both choices are the same in the sense that they are the same kind of meat—steak. Jim, however, prefers hot dogs. Although hot dogs are another (*heteros*) meat, they are not another (*allos*) of the same kind as rib eye and T-bone.

Jesus said the coming Holy Spirit would be the same kind (*allos*) of Counselor as he had been. The disciples should not expect anything different!

The Greek word for "Counselor" combines two words, one meaning "alongside" and the other meaning "called." So the Holy Spirit would be called alongside believers just as Jesus had been alongside them. He would be their helper, their teacher, their strength, their comfort.

It is unthinkable that Jesus would have abandoned his disciples when they disappointed him. He did not forsake them when they experienced lapses of faith or showed disloyalty or lost their temper or tried to keep others from him or exhibited shameless self-ambition or rebuke him because he said he would suffer and die. Why, then, would anyone think the Holy Spirit might leave a believer? After all, the Holy Spirit is another Counselor of the same kind as Jesus.

As the Counselor, the Holy Spirit has been called alongside every believer. He comforts us in our sorrow, teaches us God's will, challenges us to obey God's will, strengthens and equips us to do God's will, convicts us when we violate God's will. When we are unfaithful, he is still faithful. He will never leave our side.

Didn't Jesus promise that the Holy Spirit would be with us *forever*? His promise carried no conditional clauses. There are no riders to Jesus' promises, nor can we interpret "forever" to mean less than forever.

During my college years, I met many students who believed the Holy Spirit belonged only to Christians who had "prayed through" to receive him. They also believed his stay might be temporary. A sinning Christian, they said, could lose the Holy Spirit. I believed such thinking was strangely out of tune with Jesus' promise that the Spirit would be with believers forever (John 14:16).

Furthermore, Jesus told his disciples the Spirit "will be in you" (v. 17). This indwelling is not a reward for asking for the Spirit or for staying in a faith relationship with Christ; it is a gift to every believer listed in the will Jesus outlined in John 14.

The apostle Paul taught this truth. In Romans 8:9 he wrote, "And if anyone does not have the Spirit of Christ, he does not belong to Christ." We may safely say, therefore, that only unbelievers do not have the Holy Spirit, and by contrast, all believers (those who belong to Christ) have the Spirit.

But how long will you and I, as believers, belong to Christ? Forever! Jesus promised that we will never perish and that he will not let us slip from his hand. To borrow an advertising slogan, *we are in safe hands with Jesus.*

It may also help us to understand that the Spirit will never leave a believer under any circumstances if we know why the Spirit lives in each believer. He has taken residence in us so that he may perform a great work in us, namely, the work of transforming us into the image of Christ. Because that gracious work is a lifelong one, the Holy Spirit will live in us for the rest of our days.

Paul attributed this transforming work to the Spirit when he wrote, "And we, who with unveiled faces all reflect the Lord's glory, are being transformed into his likeness with ever-increasing glory, which comes from the Lord, who is the Spirit" (2 Cor. 3:18). In a similar vein, he credited the Spirit with interceding for us according to the will of God, which he defined as God's marking us out to be "conformed to the likeness of his Son" (Rom. 8:26–29).

Have you known any quitters? A golfer may set the goal of breaking one hundred but gives up golf after trying for years to reach his goal. A dieter may choose to shed eighty pounds but, after eating low-carb food for a couple of months, return to a diet rich in french fries, big-bun burgers, and pecan pie. A would-be author may plan to write a three-hundred-page novel but abandon the plan when she runs out of ideas on page five. However, the Holy Spirit cannot and will not fail to finish the work he came to do in us.

Writing to the believers at Rome, Paul described the Spirit's work of conforming Christians into the image of Christ as an accomplished fact. Sharing God's perspective, he explained, "And those he predestined, he also called; those he called, he also justified; those he justified, he also glorified" (8:30). We may be confident, therefore, that the Holy Spirit will never leave us. His work is far too important to abandon.

God did not design the Christian life to be one of worry. He gave each of us the Holy Spirit to assure us, to keep us on the path of righteousness, and to escort us to heaven. Instead of doubting that he is with us for the entire pilgrimage, we ought to cooperate with him and rely on him to make the pilgrimage satisfying and successful.

NOTES

1. See appendix A for a summary analysis of Paul's epis-
   tles (download appendixes at
   www.cookministries.com/misconceptions).
2. See appendixes B–E (downloadable off the Internet at
   cookministries.com/misconceptions). I argue that
   Jesus will rapture his bride and carry her to heaven (see
   John 14:1–2; 1 Thess. 4:13–17; Eph. 5:25–27). It is my
   belief that during the ensuing tribulation on earth,
   some will believe in Jesus as the Messiah, but many will
   reject him. When he returns from heaven with his
   bride to enter the kingdom, the believers converted
   during the tribulation, enter the kingdom as his invited
   guests.
3. C. I. Scofield, ed., *The New Scofield Reference Bible* (New
   York: Oxford University Press, 1967), 1324.

Additional copies of *It's a God Thing and Other
Popular Christian Misconceptions*
are available wherever good books are sold.

※

If you have enjoyed this book, or if it has had
an impact on your life,
we would like to hear from you.

Please contact us at:

VICTOR BOOKS
Cook Communications Ministries, Dept. 201
4050 Lee Vance View
Colorado Springs, CO 80918

Or visit our Web site:
www.cookministries.com

Victor®
The Bible Teacher's Teacher